A Guide to Model Making and Taxidermy

Born in Holland in 1933, Leo Cappel holds a diploma of Industrial Arts and Crafts from Amsterdam having gained experience as an art teacher and a free-lance industrial designer of furniture, plastic boats and jewellery.

He came to New Zealand in 1959 and took up a position at the Canterbury Museum in Christchurch, making diorama-type displays for country schools for the Education Department. Since 1964 he has been Preparator to the Auckland Institute and Museum, and has written several articles on preservation techniques.

A Guide to Model Making & Taxidermy

A comprehensive manual for sportsmen and teachers,
for model railway enthusiasts and other hobbyists

LEO J. CAPPEL

Preparator to the Auckland Institute and
Museum, Auckland, New Zealand.

Photographs by ARNE LOOT

A.H. & A.W. REED WELLINGTON SYDNEY LONDON

First published 1973
Reprinted 1974

A.H. & A.W. REED LTD
182 Wakefield Street, Wellington
51 Whiting Street, Artarmon, NSW 2064
11 Southampton Row, London WC1B 5HA
also
29 Dacre Street, Auckland
165 Cashel Street, Christchurch

ISBN 0 589 00727 0

Set on IBM Composer by A.H. & A.W. Reed Ltd, Wellington
Printed and bound by Kyodo Printing Co. Ltd, Tokyo

Dedication

To Colin, who has been waiting
for a long time to try it all.

Contents

About this book

In this well-illustrated craftbook the author has provided a clearly detailed guide for the modelmaking amateur and enthusiast, as well as filling a gap for museum workers and natural history students.

The balance between professional skill and pleasure is amply illustrated by Leo Cappel's informative, step-by-step approach to his models and the effective results of his work shown in the accompanying photographs. The reality and attention to detail in the models illustrated will inspire the amateur modelmaker to diversify and perfect his modelling.

A valuable section on the historical background of the art of taxidermy introduces the trophy hunter or natural history enthusiast to the preservation of animals and plants for presentation in natural lifelike habitat. Photographs of finished models of animals and trees give ample evidence of the author's experience and skill, as does the clarity of his description of methods and materials used. Vital information on wildlife legislation in Australia and New Zealand for the amateur's guidance is contained in an appendix.

For school, museum or home use, this book will provide the impetus for many hours of creative pleasure for those interested in models and manikins.

Foreword

By E.G. Turbott, Director,
Auckland War Memorial Museum

The main aim of this book is to fill a need well-known to all museum workers and, indeed, to all engaged in the encouragement of natural history activities. This is the wish, so often expressed, for simple basic information on the methods available to the amateur student for the temporary or permanent preservation of natural history material for further study or display.

Much of Mr Cappel's book consists of an introduction to the often highly complex skills of biological and archaeological modelmaking and casting. All require craftsmanship of a high order, and Mr Cappel writes clearly and interestingly, and at the same time ensures that the information needed by the beginner is available; in some chapters he passes on to more advanced aspects, and these sections will be of much value to museum workers and others carrying out preservation and display work professionally.

With respect to the sections dealing with taxidermy, it should be stressed that there is no place today for the old-fashioned approach to natural history study; largely a matter of destroying animals—especially birds—and preserving their remains in lifelike attitudes as collectors' items (or even drawing room decorations!). While a certain amount of advanced taxidermy is still needed in modern museum display, this must necessarily be a highly specialised task, and is aimed at making the best use of every available specimen; instructions for taxidermy at the professional level must be sought in suitable manuals, and the provision of such information is not the aim of the present work.

Chapter 1

OF PHARAOHS AND TROPHIES

Long ago, before even the first pyramids were built, the ancient Egyptians began to develop the art now called taxidermy. For several thousands of years this was used only for religious purposes. The old Egyptian religions taught that the soul could survive only for as long as the body was kept intact. Therefore it was of the utmost importance for the rich and high-placed people, and in particular for the pharaoh, who was considered a deity, to be mummified after death. A variety of spices, as well as asphalt, were used to preserve the body and the more important organs. Fortunately for them this primitive process was helped by the hot, dry climate. The mummy was then concealed in a permanent grave, which later took the form of the well-known pyramids. This ancient "taxidermy" was not restricted to human subjects. Many animals that represented gods were mummified too, and hundreds of mummies of cats, bulls, crocodiles and other animals have been found.

North American Indians, to mention just one more people, made wellpreserved heads of birds and many of the smaller mammals, for ceremonial purposes, as decorations on clothing, and as ornaments.

In Europe it was not until the seventeenth century that the first crude attempts at taxidermy were made. A few specimens from this early period still exist, but we know little about how they were done, other than that the skins were preserved with spices. During the first half of the nineteenth century taxidermy really began. Explorers and scientists travelled all over the world to collect exotic birds, alligators, armadillos and whatever other weird and wonderful animals they could lay their hands on. The skins were salted and shipped home, then "stuffed" and sold in considerable numbers to collectors, museums and universities. The technique in those days was to tan the skin or to preserve it with arsenic, then sew it up and literally stuff it with wood shavings, straw or the like. And the results certainly looked like that too.

This form of taxidermy grew up at a time—now past— when birds and mammals were very widely killed for display, or simply by people wishing to keep them as curiosities. This kind of collecting has long been prevented by law, but sporting trophies and certain more common, unprotected species may still come into the hands of the taxidermist. Further information on the laws covering protected fauna is given in the appendix and *you·should read this very carefully*.

Gradually the museums employed their own preparators and the more adventurous ones started to display the birds in their natural surroundings, in habitat groups or dioramas. And thus more lifelike mounting techniques were called for.

The first really successful method that developed then is still in common use. The animal is still skinned and the skin preserved in more or less the same way as originally. An exact replica of the original body is made and instead of stuffing the skin, the preserved skin is now very carefully

A well-mounted bird like this shag looks less like a taxidermy specimen if it is displayed with a suggestion of its natural habitat.

9

arranged and sewn up around this artificial body. The step was thus made from the stuffed bird to the mounted bird. So don't ever insult a good taxidermist by asking him to "stuff" the pheasant you shot.

Since then several other methods have been developed, all of them far outside the capabilities of even the best amateur. A frog, for instance, may be slowly dehydrated in a range of alcohol baths. When it is completely water-free, the specimen is gradually impregnated with melted paraffin. If this is done properly, the final result is completely lifelike and permanent.

The following method, used for game heads, also gives excellent results. The head is skinned normally, but in this case we do not preserve the skin in any way whatsoever. At the most we can keep it in a freezer until we have made an exact copy of the skinned head in ordinary potter's clay. While this clay is still soft and wet we model the fresh skin on to it and make the whole thing as lifelike as possible, even including at this stage the glass eyes. The next step is rather surprising: the entire outside is soaked carefully in thin latex. This latex soon dries and forms a layer of natural rubber with the fur completely embedded. Once the latex is dry, the whole outside is encased in plaster of paris. Figure 1 shows a cross-section at this stage. We now remove the still soft clay from the inside and soak the whole arrangement in water for a few days. This will partly macerate the skin, which can then be peeled away easily. The fur stays firmly embedded in the latex and when we look at the inside we can clearly see the roots of the hairs sticking out of the rubber. The purpose of this rather weird-sounding method is that we can now fibreglass the whole inside and thus embed the roots of the hairs in the fibre-glass exactly where the skin used to be. When the fibre-glass has set, the plaster of paris can be broken away and the latex dissolved, or rather softened sufficiently to be combed out, in kerosene, petrol or a similar solvent. The final result after this long story is, of course, a fibreglass mount with the hair implanted in the original way, and no remains of natural skin which could go mouldy or dry out or deteriorate in any other way.

The other extreme, freeze-drying, is unfortunately rather expensive. This most modern technique relates back to the very earliest mummification, but without any of the draw-backs of shrinkage or discolouration. The animal is frozen stiff in the required position and placed straight away in a deep-freeze vacuum chamber. This machine is so designed that the specimen slowly dries out without ever thawing. During the early stages the ice inside the animal keeps it in shape and when the ice dries away the tissues have become already hard enough to retain the shape.

Most of these techniques are every bit as complicated as they sound and I would strongly advise beginners to steer well clear of them. However, most of the medium-sized birds, ranging from blackbirds to pheasants, are fairly easy to mount, and even the first effort can give reasonable results. The great idea is never to rush things along. First of all, your bird must be really fresh. If the breast feathers can be pulled out too readily you can be sure of a failure. When you have a suitable specimen, wash off any blood and then put it straight away in a plastic bag and store the bird in the deep-freeze or in the freezing compartment of the fridge. Now read through the next five chapters very carefully, so you are sure you understand every part of it. The frozen bird will keep for a considerable period and therefore there is plenty of time to buy the few chemicals, materials and tools you are likely to need.

Fish are a different matter altogether. The basic method is similar to mounting birds, but fish lack the feathers to hide any inaccuracies. Even the slightest bulges in the wrong places will really show up. What is worse, it is very difficult to get rid of the fish-oil in the skin completely, which means that after a few months your fish may begin to smell most fishy indeed. A far better idea is to make a cast of your prize catch. A good cast can give a more lifelike result than a mounted fish; it is more reliable as far as size is concerned, and can't ever go bad. To make it more attractive yet, a cast is easier and quicker to make too. Again, freeze your fish before you go out to buy the materials.

The most important requirement for becoming a good taxidermist is to know the live bird. A well-mounted bird placed in a reconstruction of his natural environment can look superb. However, a bird in an unnatural pose, even when in its right surroundings, can look just as much out of place as a seagull in a dense forest. So, if you are interested in good taxidermy, take your camera and your fieldglasses and go out and meet the birds as often as you can.

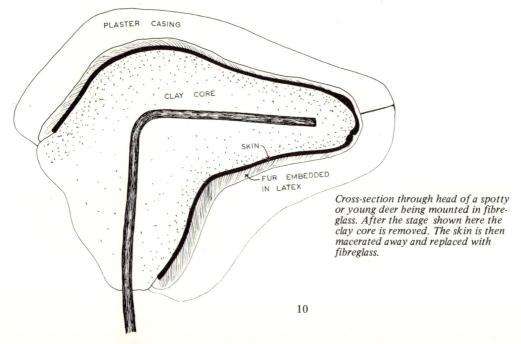

PLASTER CASING

CLAY CORE

SKIN

FUR EMBEDDED
IN LATEX

Cross-section through head of a spotty or young deer being mounted in fibre-glass. After the stage shown here the clay core is removed. The skin is then macerated away and replaced with fibreglass.

Chapter 2

WE SKIN A PHEASANT

Birds form reasonably easy subjects for taxidermy, as their feathers to some extent hide slight inaccuracies in mounting. For our first efforts we should restrict ourselves to medium-sized birds, not smaller than a blackbird, and preferably not bigger than a pheasant. The smaller birds have, of course, a rather delicate skin and are a bit tricky to handle until we have some experience. Also seabirds should be avoided for a start, as they have a more oily skin, which is difficult to clean.

The most important consideration is that almost all our native birds are protected, and rightly so. Most introduced birds are not protected, or may be hunted during the season. A very suitable bird for the first trial is the pheasant, which will not only give a nice trophy but a pleasant meal as well.

To obtain good results it is absolutely essential that the bird is really fresh. A clear indication of how long a bird has been dead is the condition of the eyes as these soon cloud over and shrink. If you have any doubts, pull on the feathers around the eyes and on the abdomen. If the feathers in those areas can be pulled out at all easily then it is better to discard the bird than to be disappointed by the results later on.

When a suitable bird has been obtained we must first of all make colour notes. Lay the bird down on a sheet of strong white paper and arrange him in a good, lifelike pose. The outline can be traced accurately on the paper. With wax crayons or paint we reproduce the exact colours of bill, eye, legs and any fleshy part in this outline drawing. The feathers themselves are quite colour-fast, but the other parts will fade very soon after death. This drawing will therefore not only help us to mount the bird in a lifelike position, but, even more important, we would not be able to touch up the final mount without these colour notes.

Any blood is now to be washed off; usually lukewarm water is sufficient, but if the bird is very soiled or the blood badly dried up a little washing soda can be added. In extreme cases a 5 per cent solution of hydrogen peroxide will solve the problem. With a thin pair of forceps we plug possible holes in the skin with cotton wool and do the same with the nostrils. If we do not already have all the materials and tools the bird must be wrapped in a plastic bag and frozen at this stage.

When all the materials have been collected and possible visitors warned that we shall be away for the weekend, we are ready to start. A bird which has been kept frozen should be taken out of the freezer the evening before to thaw out. With a freshly killed bird rigor mortis sets in fairly soon and it is easier to wait until this stiffness is gone again. First tie a strong cotton thread through the nostrils and around

the bill, leaving the loose ends of the thread as long as the body itself. Next the bird is laid on his back, with the head to the left. With the forceps in our left hand we gently part the feathers on the breast and abdomen in a straight line to the tail. It is easy to find the tip of the breastbone somewhere in the middle of the body. This is the point where the first incision is made. Use a scalpel with a new, slightly round-tipped blade. Make sure you never cut deeper than just the skin. While we keep parting the feathers with the forceps in our left hand we continue this incision along the abdomen from the tip of the breastbone to very near the anus.

If we make the incision too deep and cut through the abdominal wall it can be a bit messy, but by cutting through the skin only, very little fluid will come free, and this small amount of fluid can be absorbed all the time we are skinning by sprinkling on some dry borax powder; any excess can be wiped away with cotton wool. Borax, however, is poisonous, so if we want to eat the bird as well as mount it we have to use corn meal or potato flour instead. The skin is now gently worked free of the body, pushing and pulling with the fingers or the blunt end of a scalpel handle. Only rarely will it be necessary to use the scalpel blade. When we work this way down the body and towards the tail we soon reach the upper legs and the base of the tail. The legs are cut off at the joint. Never cut or break the bones, as we need these to give the correct length to the legs of the mounted bird. Work loose the skin around the whole top of the leg and then cut the leg clean along the body, severing it at the joint itself. The tail is treated in more or less the same manner. Leave just a little bit of the tail attached to the skin. If you leave too much it will go bad, but if nothing is left the tail feathers will fall out.

Half the body is now free, the skin hanging inside-out with the tail somewhere along the head of our bird. Care should be taken that no feathers are damaged and the skin is not stretched. By sprinkling on just a little borax occasionally we can keep everything clean and dry. When the wings are reached we detach them at the shoulder joints in the same way as we cut off the legs. It is quite an easy matter to get some more space by taking the wings from the outside in the left hand and pushing the skin back over them with the right. More or less the way one pulls off a glove.

By now the head is disappearing in the inside-out skin. Our pheasant has a nice wide neck skin but some other birds, ducks for instance, have a head that is too big for their neck. In that case we have to make a second incision, from the top of the head a little way down the back of the neck. After that it will be easy going until the head is reached, when we have to be very careful again. Birds may not show ears from outside, but they do have ears all the same, and they often prove the most difficult part of the skinning. The entire ear lining must be pulled clear of the head with a pair of small, blunt-tipped forceps. Coming to the eyes we may not find it quite as tricky, but it still pays to be very careful not to cut into the skin or damage the eyelids. Skin clean down to the bill, but never on any account cut the skin from the bill. The actual skull will be left in the final mount and if the skin were cut free of the bill it would be practically impossible to get it back on, so work down to where the skin joins the bill, but not a fraction further.

The only step left of the skinning proper is to cut off the head at the base of the skull. The body can go into the fridge for an hour or so while we clean the skin.

Cleaning the skin is a tedious job but absolutely essential, as the preservative will not act through fat or other tissues left inside the skin. The legs are pushed up through the skin to the heel joint. This is the joint where with most birds the bare part of the leg begins. Cut through the tendons near this joint and scrape away all the flesh. Remember the size and shape of these muscles or make a quick sketch of the leg. This will be useful later on. The wings are given the same treatment, so only clean bones remain attached to the skin. Now the skin itself has to be scraped clean. Use a blunt knife for this job, or a grapefruit knife. The blade of a coping saw can also be used. Whatever tool you select, always scrape away from the tail; if you scrape in the direction of the tail you will work the feathers loose and you end up with a bald bird.

The skull will also need thorough cleaning. Again remember the shape before you start cutting. All muscles, tongue, the eyes and so on are trimmed away with the scalpel until only clean bones are left. Through the hole at the base of the skull the inside of the skull is scraped clean with a special tool, the brain spoon. One can buy a dental probe of a suit-

The hardest and most difficult part of the work is now finished and the skin is ready to be washed and preserved. Usually it is sufficient to wash the skin in lukewarm soapy water. Don't use any of the modern washing powders—just mild soap flakes. It may take some time to rinse the soap out afterwards, but we must keep rinsing until the water stays clean. If there is any soap or dirt left the feathers of the finished bird won't fluff up too well and he will look a bit ill.

Some birds have a rather oily or greasy skin, in particular seabirds, and need stronger treatment: instead of soapy water a commercial dry cleaning fluid may be used, but better results are obtained with a mixture of four parts benzine to one part commercial alcohol. This mixture gives off highly inflammable vapours, as does cleaning fluid, and should therefore always be used out of doors. Do not smoke while using it. After using this degreasing fluid the feathers must be dried thoroughly before the skin goes in the preservative.

Most professional taxidermists use arsenic mixtures as the main preservative, but as arsenic is quite as dangerous as its reputation tells us, it is far better to use a saturated borax solution instead. Borax is a poison too, but not by any means as potent. Add about 50 grams of borax *powder* (borax crystals are never used in taxidermy) to 1 litre of cold water, or 2 ounces to a quart, and stir till most of the borax has dissolved. This solution can be used over and over again. The skin is entirely submerged in the solution and left to soak for about half an hour.

If everything was cleaned and degreased properly the skin will now be sufficiently preserved. Take it out by the bill so that all the feathers will fall into place nicely and let it drip out. The skin is now spread out on some newspapers with

Brainspoon.

able shape, or make a brain spoon from a piece of iron wire hammered flat at one end and bent and filed into a spoon shape. Keep the scraping edge sharp.

When there are no traces left of flesh or other tissues the skin is turned right side out again. To do this without damage we gently pull the end of the long thread which we had tied around the bill until we can grasp the head.

the feather side up and a handful of dry borax powder sprinkled over it. This will absorb excess moisture. The resulting sloppy paste is wiped off, always working with the feathers so they are not damaged. Keep repeating this with fresh dry borax until the feathers are just barely damp and begin to fluff, and the borax stays dry.

We now have a fully preserved skin, ready to be mounted.

Chapter 3

THE MANIKIN

What is called the manikin by the taxidermist is nothing but a replica of the body. This manikin can be made of a variety of materials. One of the best is balsa wood but a hard block of turf, excelsior or plasterer's tow, or even a fine grade of woodwool are also suitable.

We can already start making the manikin, and possibly even finish it, while the skin is soaking in the borax solution.

The first step is to take accurate measurements of the original body that was kept to serve as a model for the manikin: length, width, depth and circumference in different directions. Make an outline drawing and take all details of the neck.

If we use balsa or turf, just carve as accurate a copy as

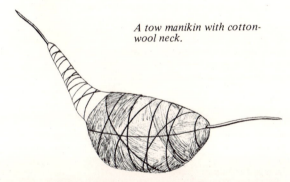

A tow manikin with cotton-wool neck.

you can of the body without the neck. The neck cannot be carved out of rigid material as we have to shape it after the bird is mounted. Sandpaper it down to as smooth and clean a shape as possible. It does not matter if the manikin is a fraction smaller than the original body, but on no account must it be larger. Compare regularly with the original body. When we are satisfied with the result the exact location of the neck and of the places where the wings, legs and tail were cut off have to be marked clearly on the manikin.

Many taxidermists use tow or fine woodwool with excellent results. Tow should be slightly damp to make the job easier. Just wrap it tightly like a flattish, elongated ball of wool with one side more or less straight—see the drawing. When this ball is about three-quarters the size of the original body, we take a piece of strong galvanised wire, several centimetres longer than the entire bird, and grind a sharp point on each end. This wire is held against the straight side of the ball and we go on wrapping until the size is just right. The wire is incorporated in the manikin as a kind of backbone, with one end sticking out as neck and the other as tail.

Strong cotton thread is now wrapped around the whole manikin in every direction and small wads of tow or woodwool included wherever necessary until the whole ball forms a hard, tight and exact copy of the original body.

With a turf manikin the backbone wire can often be pushed through from the front to give the same result, but balsa is too dense for this. In that case we have to cut

separate wires for neck and tail. Drill a small hole in the right place, fill this with glue and push the wires in as deep as they will go. If at all possible push the wire through so deeply that it comes out at the underside. The end is then bent back to form a hook and the wire pulled back so that this hook becomes anchored in the wood. Make sure this hook does not protrude above the surface.

All that remains to finish the manikin is the building up of the neck. Rub a piece of beeswax along the neckwire to give it some grip. Thin layers of cotton wool are now wrapped evenly and very tightly around the wire to the exact size of the neck. Most birds have a tapered neck, so refer to the original all the time. A little extra cotton wool is wound around the part of the wire that will later go inside the skull, just thick enough to fit through the hole at the base of the skull.

With this job done we are ready for the actual mounting.

13

Chapter 4

A BIRD IS ASSEMBLED

Ideally we ought to start mounting as soon as the skin is fully preserved, but if the making of the manikin takes longer than we expected the skin has to be moistened occasionally with borax solution to keep it soft and pliable.

The skin is now pulled inside out once more. The inside of the skull is filled with potter's clay and all the flesh we have trimmed away earlier is replaced with clay too, and carefully modelled. A few wads of cotton wool are wetted in borax water, squeezed out again and used to fill up the eye sockets. Before pulling the skin right side out again, we can make the skull a little more slippery by painting on some body paste. There are many different recipes for body paste, but for our purpose a good quality dextrine, made up with boiling water, a minute quantity of carbolic acid, and possibly a little whiting mixed in to give it more body is quite sufficient.

When we pull the skin back the right way, using the cotton thread around the bill as we did before, we must take care that the skin of the head falls naturally around the skull. Look from the front to see whether the eyes are level and watch for any folds or twisting of the skin. Any adjusting is done by gently pushing and stroking; never pull on the feathers.

Now we have to cut four more pieces of wire. The thickness depends on the size of the bird: too thin a wire and the bird will be wobbly or, worse, may not be able to stand up at all, and if it is too thick we shall not be able to push the wire through the legs without splitting the skin. The length of the leg wire must be about 7 to 8 cm (3 inches) plus the length of the leg, plus the thickness of the body. The wing wire is made a little over the length of the bony part of the wing plus the thickness of the body. As with the neck wire, each end is ground to a very sharp point.

In front of us we must now have: the skin, ready to be mounted, four pieces of sharpened wire, the finished manikin, the outline drawings which we made for a start and also a needle and thread, some cottonwool, body paste, scissors, forceps and a pair of pliers.

First to be wired are the wings. Carefully insert the wire along the wing bones and well in between the finger bones of the wing. With cotton thread, this wire is tied on to the bones and cotton wool wrapped around both the wire and the bones to the exact size and shape of the muscles cut away earlier. The cotton wool is held in place with strong thread, in the same way as the neck was finished when the manikin was made. Some body paste is painted on the cotton wool and the wings are brought back right side out. When the skin has been arranged properly and the wing feathers are falling naturally in place the wings can be bent into the right shape.

The free end of the wire is bent at right angles to the wing so that if the folded wings were to be held against the body the ends of the wing wires would poke straight through the manikin. The wings are wired from the inside out, taking care that the wires do not penetrate the skin. The legs, however, are wired from the outside, leaving about 5 cm (2 inches) sticking out under the feet. The proper place to insert the wire is under the foot so the wire will slide along the rear of the bones. Make sure the wire is just thin enough to go through the leg without breaking the skin. As with the wings, all the muscles which were cut away are replaced with cotton wool and finished with body paste before arranging the skin on the upper leg.

Although it is not necessary, a little body paste can now be painted on the neck of the manikin to make it slide easier; not too much, as we don't want to soil the feathers. The manikin is then brought into the skin with the neck wire through the hole in the base of the skull and out through the top of the skull. The manikin must be brought up as far as it goes so the head rests firmly on the cotton wool neck. As with the wings and legs, arrange the skin of the neck smoothly, without folds so the feathers fall naturally. The sharply pointed free ends of the wing wires must be inserted at the marked spots into the manikin and pushed right through. With a bird the size of a pheasant there ought to be about 25 mm (1 inch) of wire poking through the other side of the manikin. With a pair of pliers this end of the wire is bent round and hooked back into the manikin, thus anchoring the wire securely in place.

With the bird lying on its back and its legs sideways the leg wires are inserted at the marked spots and secured in the same way.

This leaves only the tail to be attached to the manikin. If we have made a manikin with tail wire then this wire should now be bent somewhat over the back of the bird so the pointed end can be pushed through the tail from the inside out. Be careful to let the wire come out in the centre of the tail, below the main tail feathers, as it would be easy to push out a feather by wiring into a shaft. Slide the tail along the wire while straightening this out until it sits in the right place against the manikin.

An alternative way is to make a manikin without tail wire. In that case the tail is secured by holding it in the right position and then inserting a sharp tail wire from the outside and as deep as it will go into the body. This method is easier, but, of course, is not as strong.

The legs are bent in shape and any inaccuracies where the legs were hooked up on the manikin can be filled up with tiny wads of cotton wool. Use forceps and keep checking from the outside, so that it does not become lumpy. By now the bird should really begin to look like a bird again.

The sewing up is actually quite easy, provided we start at the tail end and each stitch is done from the inside out, otherwise the thread is bound to catch feathers and pull them into the skin. The feathers are kept clear of the stitching with the forceps.

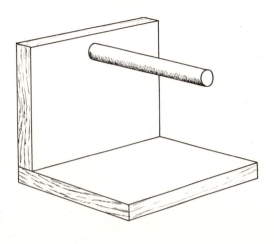

A temporary birdstand.

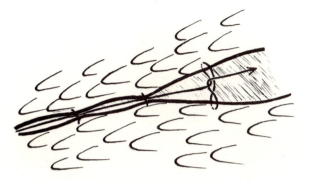

Sewing up the skin.

It is impossible to give the bird a natural pose if he cannot stand freely, so if we have not already made a permanent base it is now necessary to make a temporary stand for him. At this stage we must keep a clear picture in mind of the natural habitat. Don't ever put a ground bird on a branch, or a tree bird on a flat board.

One of the most common mistakes of the beginner taxidermist is to put the feet in the wrong positon and this is why it is so important to go out to the fields and watch the live birds. Watch how they walk and how they fly, how they put their feet and how they hold their head when they look for food; watch whether they keep their legs straight or with the heels somewhat down, whether they perch on horizontal branches or climb up and down the more upright ones. In other words, get to know your bird and if possible take several photos from close up or with a telephoto lens.

If you are unfortunate enough to have to mount a bird before you know its habits, you will have to find a number of really good photographs. There are many good photographic books available which are well worth acquiring.

A piece of timber of say 30 x 15 cm (12 x 6 inches) makes a suitable temporary stand for a ground bird, and a piece of dowel of the right diameter, mounted as shown in Figure 5, is all that is needed for a tree bird. Drill two holes in the

board or the dowel, the right distance apart, to hold the loose end of the leg wires and the bird can stand up.

Now the artist in us will get his chance because we have to take this still slightly bedraggled-looking "stuffed" bird and sculpt it into a piece of taxidermy art, making it look like a live bird. Most birds keep their neck in a sort of S curve when they are standing, so bend his neck, legs and tail until the whole pose looks right from every angle, referring all the time to the outline drawings and to photographs. With rust-proof long pins the wings are pinned in position. These pins will be removed again in a few weeks, so use as many as convenient.

When every detail of the pose looks natural most of the neckwire sticking out of the top of the head is cut off, leaving about 1 cm (½ inch). Cut two strips of thin cardboard, from an old cereal box for instance. These strips are bent or folded to fit across the tail and pinned together, clamping the tail feathers in between—see drawing.

By gently blowing and wherever necessary lifting with a needle, the feathers are finally arranged and made to fall naturally in place. Again: observe the live birds; they do this very often and know exactly how to do it properly.

Soft cotton thread is wrapped around the bird to keep every part in place while the skin dries, and a thread around the bill will keep this closed.

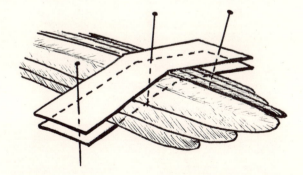

Pinned together strips of cardboard hold the tail in shape during drying.

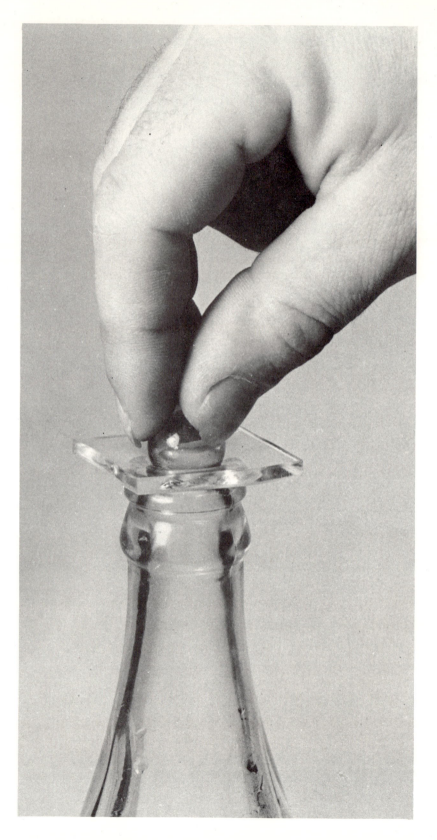

Pushing the hot, limp perspex into the neck of a bottle with a new glass marble will give it the right shape for an eye.

Chapter 5

MAKING EYES

Often far more difficult than the actual mounting of our bird is the procuring of good taxidermy eyes. One cannot just go to a shop and buy some, and if you ring the local taxidermist, provided there happens to be one, he is quite likely to say, "Sorry, I am rather low on eyes myself just now." Although good eyes of the right size and colour are obtainable in the USA or Germany, it may not be easy to import these into other countries.

Fortunately there are some reasonable substitutes that can be used for small birds. Many of the smaller birds have very dark brown or even blackish-brown eyes, for instance the goldfinch. Glass beads of the right size and colour can then be quite effective. Some ducks have yellow-brown or reddish-brown eyes and if you are lucky you may find some toy animals' eyes of the right shade.

Many times, however, we may have to make eyes ourselves. (The bright orange eyes of a pheasant are not normally found in teddy-bears.)

What we need is a very thin piece of clear perspex, an electric hotplate, some small marbles and beads of different sizes, a few medicine bottles with necks of different widths, a fine fretsaw, a very fine sable brush (00 is the best), some oil paints, glue and thin cardboard: a strange selection of materials perhaps, but easy enough to get.

Perspex is strong and rigid at normal temperatures, but becomes limp like a sheet of rubber when heated to well above the boiling point of water. Overheating, however, first causes little bubbles to appear, then the perspex turns yellow, next brown, and finally you end up with a useless black lump.

The whole eyeball is much larger than one normally realises; the visible part usually does not comprise more than about a quarter section of the eye. We shall make only a little larger section than will be visible but, of course, the curvature must be right. To make our pheasant eyes we select a bead which, if we were to add the thickness of the perspex, would be just about the size of the eyeball. Choose a medicine bottle with a neck just narrow enough so the bead will not fall through.

With the fretsaw, cut two squares of perspex about 25 mm (1 inch) in diameter, turn the hotplate on low and heat these pieces until they are limp. This will take some time as perspex is a poor conductor of heat, but it just cannot be speeded up by turning the hotplate higher. Once the perspex is really floppy take the first piece, lay it quickly (otherwise you burn your fingers and the perspex cools down) on top of the bottle and press it down immediately with the bead. After a few minutes of bead

pushing the perspex will have cooled down properly and will keep its new shape permanently. If anything goes wrong, if for instance the perspex was not hot and limp enough, or you let go of the bead before it had cooled down sufficiently – just put it back on the hotplate and try again.

The result of this rather primitive moulding process is a slightly crumpled square in the middle of which is a perfect, shiny "blank" of an eye. For something bigger, the eye of an opossum for instance, a glass marble and a correspondingly bigger bottle work very well, but for really big eyes—those of a swordfish—we get the best results by pushing the perspex in shape with a lightbulb and a jamjar.

The actual eye blanks should now be cut out of the square, but take your time: if you try to cut it too fast the saw blade will get warm enough to melt into the perspex.

The eyes are always painted on the inside, but to get as much life and depth in the eyes as possible the pupil should be left clear and unpainted. The eyes will later be backed by black cardboard and will look much better that way. Use only good quality artist's oil paints. A few small tubes are enough: cadmium yellow, cadmium scarlet, burnt umber and ivory black. Only very rarely does one come across eye colours that cannot be mixed out of these four colours.

As it comes out the tube the paint is too thick to use and has to be thinned down with a little boiled linseed oil. Squeeze out 3 mm (⅛ inch) of paint on to an old saucer, dip your brush in the oil and start mixing your colour. In this case you keep your paint thickish, not thinner than necessary to brush it on. It is very good practice to leave the paint partly unmixed so that when you paint with very light, narrow strokes from the centre outwards streaks of only partly mixed colour will give a lifelike pattern in the iris. As you are painting the inside of the perspex eye, you must turn it over regularly to see what you are doing. Remember to leave a perfectly round, clear centre as pupil.

A piece of thin cardboard, of visiting card quality, has to be painted black now, but as we need a flat finish this time instead of the high gloss we get with linseed oil, we use only mineral turpentine to thin down the paint. The more turps you use the flatter the finish; if you thin it down too much you can always give it two coats.

A sable brush is worth looking after properly. Never let it sit on its hair in a jar, not even for five minutes. After use the brush is rinsed out straight away in turpentine and then washed either with soap and a drop of water, or a neutral detergent, again with a drop of water. Most detergents do not "deterge" if they are not at least a little diluted. Keep washing the brush gently on the palm of your hand until the foam shows no sign of colour, then rinse under the tap, shake off excess water and let the brush dry with the hair up in the air.

Artist oil paints take a while to dry, so it is best to put the eyes away for a few days in a dust-free place. After that cut little circles of the black cardboard, of the exact size of the eyes, and glue these with a quick-drying plastic glue against the back of the eyes. This black cardboard will suddenly bring the eyes to life. If you want to do a really good job you can waterproof the outside of the cardboard now with some black paint or shellac.

Sequence of making a perspex eye. A square of perspex is heated and given the right bulge with the "marble and bottle" technique. The iris is then painted at the inside and the eye sawn out of the square. Glueing a circle of black cardboard underneath to the rim will give the unpainted pupil its deep black appearance.

Chapter 6

FINISHING TOUCHES

It is a safe bet that by the time the eyes are ready to be used the skin of the mounted bird is already quite dry and hard. However, this is no problem as it is easy enough to relax the eyelids again. All we have to do is to wet the wads of cotton wool which we put in the eye sockets during Chapter 4 with a solution of carbolic acid. Use rubber gloves, as pure carbolic acid, or phenol as it is also called, is a highly dangerous poison that is readily absorbed even through the intact skin. For this reason buy only a small quantity of carbolic acid *crystals,* never liquid phenol. A solution of one teaspoon of the crystals to a pint of water is strong enough. Throw away the leftover solution after the job is finished and to play it safe always keep the bottle of crystals, labelled "poison", locked away in a safe place.

Any acid spilled on the skin must be washed off immediately with plenty of water.

While the carbolic acid is slowly making the eyelids more pliable again, prepare a small batch of modelling composition. This is a mixture similar to the body paste of Chapter 4, but with more body. Make a thin glue size or strong dextrine and mix in some of the carbolic acid solution. Then work in whiting or ground asbestos, a little at a time, until it is a smooth doughlike substance similar to soft potter's clay.

When the eyelids are sufficiently relaxed the cotton wool is taken out and the eye sockets are about three-quarters filled with the modelling composition. Take care, of course, not to soil the feathers. The eyes are now sidled into the eye sockets and moved into position. Dental probes are the ideal tool for this purpose, so ask your dentist to save his old probes for you.

Look at your bird from every angle, sideways, face-on and even from above to check the position of the eyes. Once they are really spot-on, not sunken or bulging, the eyelids are gently modelled in shape. Perspex scratches rather easily so the best way to move the eyes is to hook a thin probe under the eyelid and around the rim of the perspex eye.

All that remains to be done now is to touch up the colour of the legs and any bare parts of the skin, as in the face of a pheasant. Nothing looks as horribly artificial as heavily painted legs, where the paint hides the many shades and patterns of the scales and toenails.

When we refer to the colour notes which we made as soon as we got our bird we see that the legs have lost some colour already, and they will lose quite a lot more in the years to come. Get out the artist's oil paints again and mix the right colours. For the bare skin on the face the paint is diluted with mineral turpentine until it looks more like a dye than paint. This will soak a little into the skin, giving it its natural colour without making it look painted. A second coat.is always possible, but do not overdo it. For the legs, a paint mixed with turps only is too watery and dries too flat, but a little boiled linseed oil added will give it more body and also more gloss when it is dry. Very good results can be obtained by making the paint more transparent simply by mixing it with a little thin, semi-flat varnish instead of oil. If necessary a drop of turps can still be added.

Whatever paint mixture we may use, the key to success is always: paint on as thin and unobtrusive a coat as feasible.

When we mounted our bird the idea was to make it look like a normal, live bird rather than a stuffed piece of taxidermy. Many taxidermists do not seem to realise this, and if they do their customers don't, but the same applies to the stand. A brightly coloured or heavily varnished and craftily shaped stand may be in fashion for trophies, but that is exactly the impression it creates too: a dead trophy instead of a live bird, an object instead of a living being.

Only cagebirds are normally found sitting on a piece of dowel and then only because they have nowhere else to sit, so for a tree bird find yourself a nice-looking branch, not too small and of the right thickness for the bird to sit comfortably. Many fruit trees give just the right kind of branches. Let the branch dry out completely, as timber shrinks noticeably while drying. Some base board to mount the branch on is usually still necessary, but keep this unobtrusive: a square of timber painted a dark, neutral colour is best. Again be careful to avoid the imitation effect. You might say that a seagull often sits on a beach and so glue sand on a board and mount the gull on that, but the point is that sand glued on a square of timber still does not look like a beach. If instead of that you found a simple piece of driftwood and put your gull on it the result would be very different. The first will look just what it is: a mounted seagull sitting on a piece of timber with sand glued on it, whereas the latter will be a gull sitting on a piece of driftwood, as you may often see it on the beach.

What it comes down to is that you must make the stand so that one is not aware of it. This can be done by making it like the natural surroundings one is used to seeing your particular bird in, or by making the stand as simple and unobtrusive as possible.

When the stand is finished and, if necessary, treated with borer killer, two holes are drilled to accommodate the leg wires. Cut a short, narrow slot from each hole at the underside of the board or branch so the loose ends of the leg wires can be bent flat against the board instead of protruding. These bent ends are then stapled on to secure the bird.

If the toes need any further adjusting around a branch they can be relaxed by covering them for some hours with cotton wool soaked in carbolic acid solution. Use thread and pins to keep them in place while they are drying.

Finally, the bits of wire which are still sticking out from the head and the tail are cut off and the cotton threads, pins and cardboard which kept the bird in shape are removed.

And so the bird has come to life again.

Opossum. This attractive creature is common in New Zealand not only in the bush but also in settled areas where there are plantations of trees and other suitable cover. The cured skin of the opossum is used for many purposes; rugs, gloves and winter hats being among the most popular.

Chapter 7

TANNING AN OPOSSUM SKIN

For taxidermy purposes very small mammal and marsupial skins can be adequately preserved with the same borax solution that we used to treat the skin of our first bird, but borax-preserved skins are not very supple once they are dry and I would not like to advise borax for any animal larger than, say, a large hare or an opossum.

I shall describe three basic recipes for tanning an average skin. Most of the work for the cleaning and the final treatment is identical in each case, the only difference being that we can either soak the cleaned skin in the tanning solution or pickle, or the skin can be kept damp with the solution and sprinkled on sawdust, or alternatively the dry tanning mixture may be rubbed into the skin.

If the skin is wanted for an opossum rug or a fur coat there is no need to use the head, tail or feet. Never use the skin of an animal that has been dead too long; an easy way to test this is to rub him fairly strongly over the belly: if the hair comes loose then the fur will be no good.

Make one long incision along the whole underside of the body without cutting any deeper than just the skin. Then from this incision and at right angles to it, make one more cut along the inside of each of the legs as far as the wrists and ankles. Finally, make circular cuts around the wrists, ankles, neck and tail, and the whole skin can be pulled free. Don't use the scalpel or skinning knife any more than necessary; most of the work can be done by gently pulling and working the skin loose with the fingers or the blunt end of the scalpel handle.

You may want to keep the tail on the skin. In that case there should, of course, be no circular cut around the tail when you do the skinning. Proceed with the skinning in the normal way until the whole skin, except the tail, is free. Now take two smooth boards of timber a little longer than the tail, and stretch the tail out on one of them. Put the other board on top and while pressing this down firmly move the top board to and fro so the tail rolls up and down. When the skin has been worked loose properly in this way we take the two boards with the tail tightly in one hand, and by hooking the fingers of the other hand around the base of the tail we can steadily pull the tail out of its skin.

We may be out in the field and not likely to get home very soon. In that case the skin must be liberally sprinkled on the inside with ordinary cooking salt, folded double flesh side in, and then rolled up, or alternatively the rolled-up skin may be stored in a jar of methylated spirits. Very small skins may be completely tanned in methylated spirits.

The next step is called "fleshing". If the skinning is done at home we may do the fleshing straight away, but salted skins are often too dry for this. Relaxing the dried-up skin in the carbolic acid solution of Chapter 6 is satisfactory, but for best results some cooking salt should be added as well. As soon as the skin is nicely soft again the whole inside must be thoroughly cleaned of fat, flesh and other tissues to allow the tanning solution to penetrate. A small area at a time, the skin is stretched tightly over a flat or slightly curved surface with the left hand and cut and scraped clean and free of any tissue. One can buy special fleshing knives and scrapers, but a grapefruit knife will serve the purpose.

When I have a clean, well-fleshed skin, I always find it very tempting to omit the next stage, yet for good results the skin ought to be degreased now. Very efficient is a mixture of three parts white spirits or petrol and one part methylated spirits, if available, with as low a water content as possible. An hour of soaking in this mixture will do the trick. After that, some thorough washing in several changes of water will get the skin ready for the actual tanning.

To get a nice, flat rug the skin has to be nailed onto a solid wooden panel or frame, hairside down. Use small tacks, evenly spaced along the whole outside and stretch the skin so that there are no wrinkles left.

One of the oldest but still commonly used tanning agents is a mixture of three parts alum powder and one part washing soda, or a mixture of one part alum powder and two parts cooking salt. This mixture is firmly rubbed into the wet skin and left to dry slowly. The next day we brush it off, make the flesh side of the skin wet again and repeat the process. Any pinkish areas left after that have to be treated again till the skin is an even colour all over.

Instead of using alum, we can tan the nailed-up skin with the following pickle:

Water	1 litre
Non-iodised cooking salt	50 grams
Concentrated sulphuric acid	10 mils

Do not add the acid until the salt has been dissolved completely, and always store this solution in a glass or plastic container. Place the board with the skin in a level position and pour some of the pickle on the flesh side of the skin. Sprinkle a thin even layer of sawdust over it to stop the liquid from running away and then pour more pickle on. When the entire skin has been covered with the sawdust and pickle mixture spread a sheet of plastic over it so it will not dry out and leave the whole arrangement for a day.

When we preserved the skin of our pheasant, we just soaked it in a kind of tanning solution. The same can be done with skins of any size if we choose the right solution. Borax is fine for thin skins, but it will not penetrate deeply enough to tan a deerskin, for instance. A very suitable tanning pickle is made up as follows:

Pour 1 litre of boiling water over 100 grams of bran (or 1 quart of water to 4 oz of bran) and let it soak for half an hour before straining it. While this is soaking, dissolve as much non-iodised cooking salt as you can in 1 litre of cold water. When the bran-stew has been strained through a piece of linen into a plastic bucket the salt solution is also strained (to keep out the excess undissolved salt) into the same bucket; now add 6 mils of concentrated sulphuric acid and mix everything thoroughly. This pickle is very similar to the above, but acts more gently and is therefore more suitable for soaking the complete skin in.

A thin skin like an opossum skin will be properly tanned after staying in this pickle for two days; heavier skin, however, may require as much as four days.

The tanned skin is now taken out of the bath, pegged up on a board as with the previous technique, and left to drain and dry.

If we select the second tanning agent then we can move straight on to the next step. With the first and the third, however, the skin has to be dampened with the carbolic acid solution to soften it again; half an hour will be ample.

At the hardware store it is possible to purchase an oil specially prepared for leatherwork: sulphonated neatsfoot oil. Mix some of this oil with an equal quantity of hot water and shake well before painting the resulting emulsion all over

the flesh side of the fur. Again let it dry properly and dampen it once more with the carbolic acid solution. The skin is then rolled up tightly, flesh side in, and left overnight.

The most tiring part of the job is still to come: the skin has to be made pliable. The tool needed for this is very simple. Place a strong clean board of 25 mm (1 inch) timber in a big vice or clamp it horizontally against the side of a heavy table so it extends out 30 cm (1 foot) or more. The sharp edges are sanded or planed down until everything is smooth and the skin will not get caught anywhere. Rub some neatsfoot oil on it too if you wish; the whole thing must be smooth, yet not too rounded off.

Now take the skin in both hands and work it to and fro over the edge of the board with a sawing motion, stretching and bending it in every direction until the whole skin is soft and supple.

All that is left now is to clean our fur rug. The hair–but NOT the leather–is cleaned with white spirits or dry cleaning fluid, and chalk or clean sawdust sprinkled on to absorb any excess. Beat this out again with a carpet beater or a piece of plastic hose.

If you are very particular the leather can now be cleaned with a little, lukewarm, soapy water, keeping the hair dry this time.

Heavy skins might require a final dressing of neatsfoot oil and water, or even a light coat of straight neatsfoot oil, but your fur rug should be really beautiful by now.

A hunter's trophy–this head will be mounted as described in Chapter 8.

Chapter 8

GAME HEADS

Mounting an entire mammal is considerably more difficult than a bird as the manikin has to show every muscle bulging the right way for any particular pose. In particular, with short-haired mammals where inaccuracies cannot be hidden, one needs a fair understanding of anatomy to achieve life-like results. With game heads this problem is less pronounced.

The basics of skinning and tanning are the same as when making rugs. Make the first circular incision around the neck very close to the body, so there is plenty of skin to work with. The second incision is always made at the back of the neck and, in the case of a stag or ram, branches at the top to end at the antlers or horns.

Particular care must be taken with the ears, which are cut off close to the skull, and with the eyes. The cartilage in the tip of the nose is left on the skin and the lips are cut free along the jawbones.

The skin is now fleshed and cleaned as in Chapter 7, but to do this properly the lips and the eyelids must be split open from the inside so all tissues can be removed. The ears have to be pulled inside out and the cartilage removed in one piece. This cartilage is kept for later reference.

For the tanning use the bran pickle of Chapter 7 and leave the skin in this pickle for four days, with occasional stirring.

The only difference between tanning for a game head, or a full mount for that matter, and tanning a rug is that for the former the skin should keep its exact shape and size, so in this case the skin is not pegged up. Apart from that the whole process is the same.

Sometimes readymade manikins can be purchased for game heads of almost any size, but many taxidermists use the original skull to build the manikin. Take measurements and make several sketches before cleaning the skull; then cut and scrape away as much flesh and other tissue as possible; in particular the brains and the inside of the nose must be cleaned out well. Boiling in a solution of washing soda will help with degreasing. Stags' antlers will stay on the skull, but the horns of a ram can be slipped off and cleaned separately, to be glued on again after the mount is finished.

The lower jaw always comes away during the cleaning and has to be wired back on.

Now some accurate measuring must be done. The exact cross section at the base of the neck, about 50 mm (2 inches) above the first incision through the skin, has to be cut out of a 19 mm (¾ in) plank, coreboard or the like. A 6 mm (¼ in) or 9 mm (⅜ inch) iron rod is securely screwed on this base board, bent in the shape of the spine and attached inside the skull with plaster of paris. Instead of plaster a two-component plastic putty can be used successfully, such as CIP emerkit, made by Austin Carr Ltd. The rough shape of the neck, 25 mm (1 inch) or so thinner than the final measurement, is built out of fine chicken wire, stapled on to the base board and wired onto the "spine" and the skull. At this stage the sketches should be brought out: with the modelling composition used to put in the eyes in Chapter 6, both head and neck are modelled to the exact size and shape of the original; leave some extra space for lips and nose. Two pieces of aluminium sheet are cut and bent to the shape of the ear cartilage and attached in the right place. Perspex or glass eyes can be put in now and everything left to dry.

By the time the skin is fully tanned the manikin should be ready for mounting. First give the entire manikin a liberal coating of body paste (Chapter 4) and then drape the skin in place. If all the measurements were correct the skin will extend about 50 mm (2 inches) behind the baseboard. Fold this flat and nail it with plenty of cut tacks against the back of the baseboard. Gently slip the ears in place and sew up the incision. It often helps to pin the flaps of skin in place while the sewing is being done so we end up straight.

The extra space left for the lips and nose can now be filled out with fresh modelling composition and everything is pushed, pinned and modelled into place.

When completely satisfied with the results, leave the mount to dry for a few weeks.

Finally, the lips and nose are touched up with oil paint, as for mounting a bird, and the traditional varnished shield screwed against the baseboard.

Chapter 9

PREPARING SKELETONS

The bones of the skeleton in a live animal are connected by strong flexible ligaments. With careful handling, use can be made of these ligaments to keep the animal skeleton together when mounting it. When I first attempted to prepare a skeleton I was advised to let ants clean the bird in question— and they certainly cleaned it very effectively, including all those ligaments! I then realised what a considerable knowledge of anatomy was required to build an accurate skeleton out of a disorganised heap of loose bones.

Fortunately it is possible to prepare a skeleton without damaging to any great extent the connecting tissues. First of all, the animal is skinned and all flesh cut away with scissors and a sharp scalpel. The more flesh we can cut away from the bones the less messy a job we get afterwards, so it pays to take time at this stage.

With both birds and mammals, the head is then cut off at the base of the skull. With bigger mammals, the legs too may be cut off without damaging the bones.

When as much flesh as possible has been removed the entire skeleton is put in a plastic or enamel container with warm water to macerate; the warmer the water is kept the quicker and better this rotting process will be, but *on no account may the water reach boiling point* as this would separate the bones. While maceration goes on any tissues becoming soft enough are scraped or brushed away with scissors, forceps, *blunt* scalpel and toothbrush; usually the whole skeleton will be clean and still hanging together after a few days.

The final cleaning is done under water with the container sitting under a gently running tap to wash away any flesh; leave it under the tap for some time further to rinse.

Bones contain big quantities of fats and oils which must be removed. Degreasing may be done in a hot—but never boiling—weak solution of washing soda for several hours, or in white spirits with some alcohol added for at least a week. After degreasing, rinse again in running water for some hours.

The soda will have made the bones quite white but if desired the skeleton may be further bleached in 4 per cent hydrogen peroxide for two days.

The skeleton is now ready for mounting. The main support, which is essential for skeletons of almost any size is a copper, brass or galvanised iron wire or rod through the spine. It must be strong enough for general support, yet reasonably easy to bend so the shape of the spine can be adjusted afterwards. This wire is threaded through the vertebrae with just enough still protruding in front to take the skull, in the same manner as the main wire in a taxidermy manikin.

Unless the legs are wired strongly enough for the finished skeleton to stand by itself a special stand must be made to support its weight and attach it to the base. Easiest for this purpose is some strong aluminium channel, a strip with a U-shaped profile, of such a size that the spine can sit comfortably on top of the open side; bend this into a form of bridge, open side up, with the horizontal part a little shorter than the body and the verticals long enough so that the feet of the skeleton do not quite reach the floor. Slide this channel through the rib cage and push the ends of the verticals into tightly fitting holes which were drilled in a temporary base. The still-headless and slightly bedraggled skeleton now hangs with its legs on either side of the bridge with only the spine properly supported. To make the task easier the spine should be straightened out and tied bit by bit with cotton thread to the supporting channel. The rib cage is next to be tied in place; knot a thread on to the support in front of the rib cage and then to each of the ribs on one side in sequence so that when the end of the thread is tied on to the rear support the ribs are properly spaced and securely linked together. Do the same with the other side.

Lengths of strong copper wire are cut to the size of the legs, bent in approximately the right shape and temporarily tied along the leg bones. When all legs have been strengthened in this way it is easy to make the final adjustments.

If the legs have been cut off, or have fallen off during the cleaning, small holes have to be drilled through the joints so that the legs can be wired onto the pelvis and the shoulder blades with fine, non-springy brass wire.

The wings of a bird can be treated in the same manner.

Drill small holes in the joints of the jaw and wire the jaw securely to the skull. A small cork is pushed in the hole at the base of the skull and the spine wire passed through this cork.

Any final adjustments to the skeleton should be done now, and bones which may have become detached should be wired or glued on again.

Drying may take a few weeks but it must never be done in the sun, although warm dry air will help a lot. When the skeleton is completely dry it can be mounted on a permanent base and all temporary threads and wires removed.

We do not always get specimens fresh enough to cut much flesh away. We may find, for instance, a dried-up bird at the beach which nevertheless could make an interesting skeleton. In that case we have to choose a more potent process than the simple maceration. The traditional mixture is called antiformin, and is made up as follows:

Dissolve 150 grams of sodium carbonate in 250 mils of

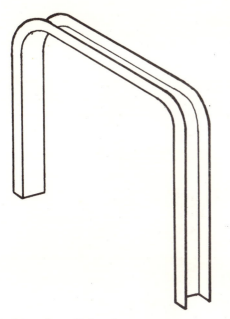

water, and 100 grams of calcium hypochlorite in 750 mils of water; mix these two solutions, stirring occasionally for two hours, then strain. Now make another solution of 180 grams of sodium hydroxide in 1 litre of distilled water and add this to the first. This mixture is called the "stock solution".

For most jobs this is diluted in the required quantity to a 10 per cent solution, i.e. 1 part stock solution to 9 parts water.

To treat a dried-out bird with antiformin, just soak it in a hot 10 per cent solution instead of macerating.

The gelatinous mass into which skin and flesh are turning is regularly brushed away until we finish with a clean skeleton.

By seeing what this mixture does to the bird one can imagine what even the 10 per cent solution would do to one's hands, *so rubber gloves are essential.*

Degreasing will not be necessary but rinsing for several hours certainly is. If desired the bones can still be bleached for half a day in hydrogen peroxide and then the skeleton is ready for mounting.

The most effective mixture to bleach old, badly yellowed bones is a thin paste of magnesium carbonate in hydrogen peroxide of 35 per cent; simply paint on a good coat of this paste and let it dry. When it is brushed off again you will find the bones nicely bleached. It is, however, not only effective but also unhealthy unless rubber gloves are used, and during the brushing off wear a dust mask or some cotton wool tied over mouth and nose with a handkerchief.

Aluminium channel is bent into a temporary support for the spine.

A cheap but reasonably efficient dustmask. The frame is made of thin aluminium and can be bent to fit the face. The filter is a layer of cotton wool sandwiched between gauze.

25

Float an aquarium in a rockpool and place the camera inside to take underwater photographs.

This underwater shot was taken through a window of the floating aquarium. For black and white photography select views with sufficient contrast and print on hard paper.

Chapter 10

PRESERVATION OF MARINE ANIMALS, REPTILES AND AMPHIBIANS

In Chapter 2 we found it quite sufficient to make a few colour notes of our pheasant after it was killed. With marine animals like fishes, crabs or starfishes we have to go one step further, or if possible even two steps. A fish will often change colour even while it is dying, and an animal like the octopus, for instance, can show very vivid changes in colour as soon as you make him excited by trying to catch him.

Photographic "colour notes" taken in a rock pool before you actually catch the animal are often far more exciting and beautiful than the preserved animal itself, and yet it is not at all difficult to take them. Any camera will do, but a reflex camera is the most suitable. My first successful underwater photos were taken with an old Agfa box camera. I managed to obtain an old lens with a focal distance of 30 cm (12 inches) which I mounted in the frame of a yellow filter in front of the normal camera lens. This enabled me to come close up to the subject.

If you want to find the focal distance of any lens, hold it up to the sun and measure at what distance from the lens the sunlight is focused into a pinpoint of light.

The only non-photographic equipment you need for taking underwater photos in a rock pool is a small aquarium, just big enough to house your camera. Simply float the aquarium in the rock pool like a little boat and place the camera inside with the lens against one of the windows. If you have a reflex camera with a viewfinder that allows you to view from above it is very simple indeed to focus on whatever you want to take and to shoot away; otherwise you have to mount a little mirror behind the viewfinder at a 45° degree angle to see what you are doing.

With an ordinary, non-reflex camera it is a little more complicated but you can still get the same results. The only difficulty is focusing; when one looks into an aquarium with water, it seems to be much less deep than it actually is, and any camera sees the same as you. My old box camera, with its 30-cm (12-inch) focal length lens attached, could "see sharp" at 30 cm (12 inches) when set at infinity. This corresponds to a real distance under water of 40 cm (16 inches). In other words, the apparent distance at which your camera must be focused is three-quarters of the real distance.

With a reflex camera you do not have to worry about this, and with any other camera you just measure the distance from the lens to the object and set your camera at three-quarters of this figure. Or, with the primitive set-up I started off with, you know at what distance objects will be in focus, add one-third to this, cut a thin stick of that length to hold in front of the camera and this measure will tell you exactly

what will be sharp in your photo.

The exposure times vary somewhat according to the light, so if you own an exposure meter put it inside the aquarium alongside the camera; otherwise play it safe and take each shot three times, one the same exposure as you would use in the air, one with one stop longer time, and the last two stops longer. With short-distance work it pays to have the diaphragm not open any wider than necessary.

Of course, there is always a risk involved: you may become so absorbed in taking underwater photos, in colour naturally, that you completely forget to catch anything, something for which the starfishes will be just as grateful as you are when you project your slides on the screen.

But that was not the original purpose, so we shall start preserving.

There are two major systems of preservation, namely "wet" and "dry". Wet preserving means that the animal is kept permanently in a glass or perspex container filled with liquid preservative. For many of the more fragile marine life forms this is the only successful way.

Dry preserving comprises a whole range of different techniques from straight taxidermy to impregnating the specimen with suitable chemicals and then drying it to give a permanent result. A technique such as the embedding of specimens in clear plastic is a form of dry preservation with some of the advantages of wet preservation—ease of handling without damage to the specimen, and no insect damage. No moulds will ever grow on it.

One of the main difficulties with marine animals is the killing. If you are too harsh, a starfish will often cast off his arms and an anemone will shrivel up into an unrecognisable lump of slime. Therefore the animal is gently put to sleep first, or as the official term goes, it is narcotised. Once the specimen is completely narcotised it can be killed and preserved.

Fishes
The best chemical to narcotise fish is tricane methanesulphonate. Make a solution of 1 gram per 4 litres of seawater, or tapwater in the case of freshwater fish. After five minutes in this solution the fish will be sound asleep. Test this by prodding him with a dissecting needle; as long as there is any reaction at all the narcosis is not deep enough.

To kill the properly narcotised fish, put it for a couple of hours in a 10 per cent solution of formalin. Pure formalin is the liquid sold at the chemist's as 40 per cent formaldehyde, so 10 per cent formalin means 1 part of that liquid to 9 parts of water.

While the fish is in the killing agent prepare the permanent storage jar: best are glass or perspex containers with at least one perfectly flat side for viewing, but any clean jar of the right size with a well-fitting glass or plastic lid will do. Cut a piece of perspex to fit in the jar; clear perspex will allow the fish to be seen from both sides, but white, black or sometimes even coloured perspex may show the fish to advantage.

The fish is now taken out of the formalin and tied on to the perspex with nylon thread. A particularly nice result is obtained if several tiny holes are drilled in the perspex behind the fish and the specimen is sewn on with the thread passing through the non-display side of the body.

As a storage liquid, 5 per cent formalin, made up with distilled water, is quite strong enough. Fill the jar to near the top and rub some vaseline or petroleum jelly on the rim before putting on the lid to improve the seal. Any labels can be written on heavy cartridge paper with indian ink and placed inside the jar.

Formalin is still one of the most commonly used preservatives, because it is cheap and can be taken along on long collecting trips in its pure form and made up when required to solutions of any strength. However, strong formalin tends to bleach the delicate colours of specimens and better results are often obtained with the following storage fluid: (Note—the narcotising and killing remain the same as above.)

Distilled water	600 mils
PEG 1500	400 grams
Formalin	20 mils

PEG or, as its full name reads, polyethyleneglycol, is a synthetic waxlike material which dissolves quite easily in water. It is available from the Shell Oil Company.

For very small specimens another storage fluid can be used:

Water	950 mils
Zinc sulphate	50 grams
Hydrochloric acid (pure)	8 mils
Sodium sulphite (crystals)	12 grams

Always add the chemicals in the order given and wait before adding the later chemicals in the list until the earlier ones have been completely dissolved.

This solution smells very strongly of sulphur dioxide and should therefore be mixed in a well-ventilated room, away from potplants. It should be made up immediately before use and as its sterilising action depends upon the sulphur dioxide which remains in solution, the finished mount must always be kept completely sealed.

One advantage of this storage fluid is that water weeds preserved in the zinc sulphate solution of Chapter 12 can, along with many other aquatic animals, be mounted together with the fish in the same jar, thus making a very attractive display.

Starfishes

Narcotising a starfish is very much a matter of patience, as strong or sudden doses of any chemical will greatly upset the specimen and make it cast off its arms. In its normal everyday life a starfish may sometimes lose one or more of its arms in a narrow escape from some undersea battle with its enemies. It will then grow new arms again fairly quickly to replace the lost ones, and when the new ones are still small will show a typical comet shape. As this should be avoided place the starfish in a deep glass container filled with just a little fresh seawater; now add a few crystals of epsom salts. The starfish will start wandering about but

will settle again after some time; then add some more epsom salts and keep repeating this every quarter of an hour or so. After an hour or more the starfish will begin to react less and less to fresh doses of epsom salts and eventually will go to sleep.

When the starfish shows no reaction to additional doses of epsom salts and it is quite certain that he is sound asleep then slowly add small quantities of 5 per cent formalin to kill and fix the specimen. Fixing in this context means to stop as far as possible any post-mortem changes. Transfer to straight 5 per cent formalin after some time and leave for a few hours to one day, depending on the size.

Using big office pins the specimen is now pinned in the right shape on to a piece of paper-covered softboard and left to dry in a warm, dark place. Put the pins askew over the arms, so that they cannot curl up while they are drying. After a few weeks he will be rigid and free of any smell. Unfortunately, starfishes lose their colour rather badly so he must be toned up again with an oil paint mixture as used for the bird legs in Chapter 6. Colour notes made from the live specimen and photographs are indispensable to get reliable results.

If the smell of formalin becomes too offensive, the room can be sprayed with a 2 per cent solution of "Alamask" Formol 10-X-M, made by May & Baker Limited; this neutralises the smell for several hours, more than long enough to finish the job.

Shellfish

If we wish to preserve the entire animal then it is again necessary to narcotise it first. This can be done with epsom salts as with the starfish, but also by sprinkling menthol onto the water in which we kept him happy, the latter also acting as killing agent; the former is to be followed by a bath in fairly strong (say 8 to 10 per cent) formalin. Snails can then be stored in the same formalin solution or in one of the other storage fluids used for fishes.

Marine slugs for that matter do not have to be narcotised but may be killed by dropping them in glacial acetic acid.

To clean the shells of most molluscs, leave the whole animal for a few hours in methylated spirits; the body then becomes solid and can be taken out easily.

Land snails belong to the molluscs too, but are better narcotised and killed by leaving them for twenty-four hours in the following mixture:

Alcohol	9 mils
Turpentine	1 mil
Water	90 mils

After that they are stored in the same manner as shellfish.

Some species of shellfish can give very attractive "mother of pearl" effects and these are most popular for jewellery and ornaments. Suitable species already show a kind of mother of pearl on the inside. The same surface may be exposed on the outside too by simply dissolving the outer layers in weak hydrochloric acid. One important warning: when we dilute any strong acid we must always slowly *pour the acid into the water*, stirring all the time with a glass rod. NEVER POUR WATER INTO THE ACID, as it would get so hot it would boil explosively and splash acid all around.

Crabs

Fresh water is a deadly poison to marine crabs, so all that is necessary to narcotise and kill them is to put them for some hours in a jar of fresh water. This will not only kill them but will also make their flesh swell after the killing, which makes the next operation easier.

The parts of the shell will have opened up slightly at the back, where body and tail join. With a small scalpel this gap is opened a little wider and with scalpel, forceps and dental probes or taxidermist's brain spoon remove as much flesh as possible without damaging the specimen. The little flesh that cannot be reached and the tissues inside the legs and tail are sufficiently preserved by soaking the cleaned crab in a 5 per cent formalin solution. But do not leave crabs in formalin for more than a day at the most.

The crab is now pinned up on softboard and dried as for a starfish.

Again, as with the starfish, a crab will lose its colour to a surprising extent, so colour notes should be made while the animal is still alive and some oil paints, this time mixed with boiled linseed oil as well, are essential.

Crabs are particularly prone to attacks by museum pests, a few species of small insects who thrive on crabmeat; the finished specimen must therefore be kept in a permanently sealed container, for instance an insect box with a glass or perspex window lid, in which is pinned a small cloth bag with some paradichlorobenzene crystals, or even a mothball.

Reptiles

Many of the bigger reptiles such as crocodiles and the bigger snakes can be mounted successfully by the standard taxidermy techniques. Smaller species, however, in particular the smaller lizards, are very difficult subjects to make into a dry mount. One good technique is the freeze-drying method described in Chapter 15, but in many cases a wet mount is the most advisable.

Whatever mounting technique we choose, the killing remains the same and is certainly easier than the catching.

The poison employed is carbon monoxide, a gas which every car owner produces in big quantities. Just put the specimen in a cardboard box with a small hole; then place this box, well shut, behind the car so that the exhaust pokes into the box through the hole, and start the motor—some five or ten minutes idling will be effective. Make sure that this is not done inside the garage but out in the open so the carbon monoxide will not be too generally effective.

As storage fluid for a wet-mounted reptile, choose one of the three given for fishes.

Amphibians

Frogs and toads, as far as they are not protected, are treated in the same way as small reptiles. To make a dry mount by taxidermy techniques is possible, but so difficult I would never advise it.

An easy way to kill a frog without using any poison is by pushing a blunt, round-tipped probe onto the spinal cord straight behind the skull with a slightly forward movement.

Just a final hint if you have freeze-dried a frog: a specimen such as a frog will look a bit chalky when it comes out of the freeze dryer and needs some further varnish treatment as mentioned in Chapter 15. A frog out of the water always looks wet and our specimen would need a high gloss varnish to get this look, but if it is intended to use the frog in an underwater display, together with fish, aquatic insects and whatever else may be found in a pool, it is a different matter, because under water nothing ever looks wet: the wet look is caused by light reflecting on a thin film of water, and under water this thin film is not there to reflect any light; so in that case paint your specimen with a mixture of flat varnish and a little oil paint.

Pinning up the still wet starfish. This specimen was in the process of growing some new arms when caught.

A simple aspirator. The mouth-tube (left) is attached to a short glass tube through the stopper, which in turn is closed inside the vial by a piece of gauze. The gauze is held in place by a very short ring of rubber hose.

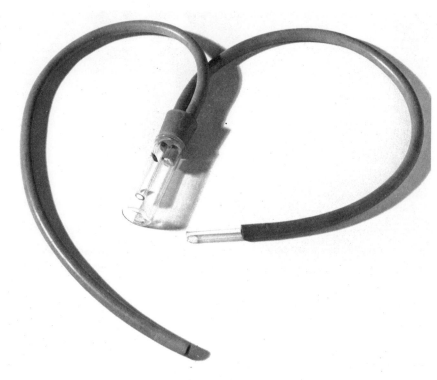

The aspirator in use. It can also be used to advantage to pick up smaller insects out of an insect net.

Chapter 11

INSECTS

Insects, and in particular butterflies, form one of the most widely-collected groups of animals, possibly second only to molluscs. Do not forget that even the biggest collection is worthless without complete data such as location, date and any other relevant particulars.

The most suitable collecting techniques vary considerably from one group to another. Butterfly nets are, of course, well known and can be used not only to catch butterflies but also to sweep through long grass and bushes to collect moths, flies, bugs, beetles, spiders and whatever else may be crawling around. Make sure you have always plenty of jars and vials to take the catch home without damage through overcrowding. Many species are best caught at night near an outside light.

Apart from true insects we can find many other arthropods such as centipedes and spiders in and under dead tree trunks or in leaf mould. A trapdoor spider we can find by digging up his tunnel. These tunnels, in tussock land and clay banks, or even in a paddock, can be very difficult to locate as they are often concealed by a carefully camouflaged, hinged trapdoor. Sometimes you find a little heap of bare soil which the spider excavated when she constructed the tunnel, and by gently feeling around near this bare patch you can then find the trapdoor. The spider lives underneath this trapdoor with possibly a nest of young ones deep down.

Many small insects live under stones and can be picked up easily with an aspirator. An aspirator is made of a glass vial, a cork in which we drill two holes, two pieces of 9 mm (⅜ inch) glass tube and about 1 metre (3 feet) of rubber hose.

Stick the two pieces of glass tube through the holes in the cork; with a small rubber band tie a piece of muslin over the opening of one of the tubes (see photograph), and put the cork in the vial; slip two lengths of rubber hose over the glass tubes and the instrument is ready.

To operate it, suck through the hose connected *to the muslin-covered tube*, when any small insect will be sucked through the other hose into the vial, which works like a miniature vacuum cleaner.

Narcotising and killing methods depend on the species. Bigger beetles can be thrown in boiling water, and an effective killing jar for most insects and spiders is made by putting a 1 cm (½ inch) layer of cotton wool in the bottom of a suitable jar or vial with tightly fitting lid. Pour some drops of ethyl acetate on the cotton wool. The cotton wool is then covered with a few circles of blotting paper so the insect will not get entangled in it, and the jar is ready for use.

I would very strongly advise against "professional" cyanide jars, as these are highly dangerous and completely unnecessary. A good killing jar for butterflies is made by mincing or crushing young leaves of the laurel tree, *Prunus laurocerasus*, and filling a jar for about 3 cm (1 inch) with this mince. Again put some circles of blotting paper on top. This jar is ready for use after one or two days and will remain effective for at least one season. It acts very slowly, however, and butterflies must be left in a laurel leaf jar for twenty-four hours.

Quite often, when the insect comes out of the killing

Both the laurel leaf killing jar and the relaxing box are easily improvised.

A trapdoor spider lives in a deep tunnel with a camouflaged trapdoor.

vapours. The insect is now placed on a plastic saucer in the relaxing box which must be kept closed for one day.

For the actual mounting it is necessary to buy some more special equipment: rust-proof insect pins, a sharp dissecting needle, a pair of straight and bent forceps, and some pinning boards. The latter may be bought, but can be made quite easily.

A pinning board can consist of a piece of softboard 20 x 8 cm (8 x 3 inches), on which is glued two strips of cork tile, styrocel foam plastic, softboard, or a similar material that will take pins easily. Leave a groove between the two strips of 9 to 12 mm (⅜ to ½ inch) wide and deep, depending on the size of the insect, and line the top, including this groove, with thin, shiny white paper.

When the insect is properly relaxed, without getting wet, it is ready to be pinned up. Select a rust-proof insect pin of a suitable size and push it carefully through the body. This is the most delicate part of the operation, as it is easy to damage wings or break off legs. Most insects are mounted with the pin through the middle of the thorax, the pin coming out between the first and the second pair of legs. Beetles get their pin through the righthand wing cover, near the wing base (which is where the wing is attached to the body) and bugs and cicadas through the thorax, slightly to the right of the centre.

From now on we don't touch the insect with our hands any more but handle it only by holding this pin in a strong pair of bent forceps. Now pin it in the groove of the pinning board with the wings level with the top of the board. Cut several strips of smooth paper, 6 mm (¼ inch) wide and long enough to go across the wings. With an ordinary office pin, one of these strips is pinned down by the end slightly in front of one of the wings. With the sharp point of the dissecting or arranging needle placed behind one of the veins, the wing is pushed forward underneath the paper strip into the right position, and while we hold it there the free end of the strip is secured behind the wing with another pin. Always use forceps to push the pins into place.

A good arranging needle can be made of a sewing needle and the shaft of a worn-out, very fine paint brush. Cut off or pull out the hair and push the eye-end of the needle with a drop of glue into the ferrule of the brush.

jar, it will be too rigid for easy mounting. In that case it must be relaxed first. Commercial relaxing tins are usually made of zinc, but a good polythene lunchbox is just as suitable. A layer of cotton wool, felt or even sand goes on the bottom. Some crystals of thymol put in the middle will prevent moulds on the insect, and some boiling water poured on the cotton wool will provide the relaxing water

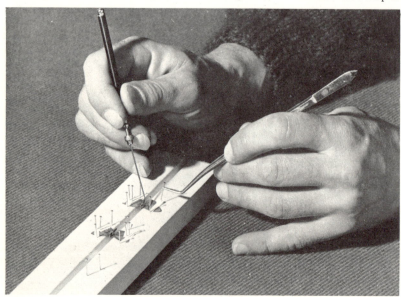

Use curved forceps and a sharp dissecting needle to arrange insects on the pinning board.

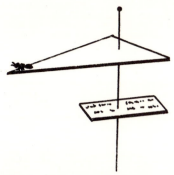

Very tiny insects are glued to the tip of smooth cardboard triangles.

When all the wings have been pinned down in this manner the legs and antennae are arranged, and if necessary kept in place with pins too. Even the abdomen may need support.

Let the whole set-up dry for one or two weeks until the insect is rigid.

Before mounting, *soft-bodied* insects must be slit open along the underside of the abdomen with a fine scalpel, or better, with a very fine pair of scissors, like surgical "iris scissors". The soft parts inside are then removed with the forceps and replaced with cotton wool or properly modelled beeswax.

Many insects are too tiny to be mounted on an insect pin and are glued instead on the sharp point of a small triangle cut out of cardboard of visiting-card quality. This triangle is then stuck on a pin for the final mounting in an insect box.

Caterpillars, larvae of aquatic insects and the like are difficult to mount by traditional methods and can be preserved more successfully by the freeze-drying method of Chapter 15.

Mounted insects must always be stored in special insect-proof glasstopped boxes as otherwise they are bound to be eaten by other insects, or to get damaged in some other way. These insect boxes have a paper-lined bottom of cork or similar material so the insect can be pinned in easily on the pin on which it was mounted originally.

Before putting it in the box, however, we stick a tiny card on the same pin with name, locality, date and any other particulars written on it in indian ink.

It is advisable, as an extra safety measure, to include in the box a little muslin bag on a pin with some crystals of paradichlorobenzene, to keep possible insects out.

Finally, insects must always be stored in the dark as their colours, particularly in the case of butterflies, fade easily. Even long exposures to artificial light are harmful, and contrary to the behaviour of many paints and textile dyes, which are most susceptible to U.V. light, the colours of insects can be badly bleached by the heatrays of an ordinary incandescent lamp.

Two sprays of trees, native to New Zealand, preserved several years ago in PEG.

A small waterweed, kept in the zinc sulphate storage fluid.

Chapter 12

PRESERVATION OF BOTANICAL MATERIAL

It is often desirable to produce three-dimensionally preserved plants rather than flat herbarium specimens. There are several techniques for this but they all have one thing in common: the plants must be absolutely fresh.

In general, plants collected in autumn preserve best but this is not always possible. In any case they should never be picked during the hottest period of the day. When collecting, put the specimens straight away into a special tin or plastic bags and keep them cool. Once a plant starts to wither it will not make a good specimen.

As with animals, plants can be either dry-preserved or put in jars as fluid mounts.

The main difficulty with plants is to preserve the green colour. This problem has been overcome to a great extent in the following procedure.

The fresh plants are fixed for from four hours to one day, depending on the thickness of the leaves, in this

Fixative

Sodium water glass (commercial)	10 mils
Water	990 mils

After fixing the plants are rinsed in clean water and put straight into the

Storage Fluid

Zinc sulphate (commercial)	50 grams
Copper sulphate (commercial)	5 grams
Hydrochloric acid (pure, concentrated)	12 mils
Sodium sulphite (crystals)	16 grams
Water	950 mils

To make a clear solution dissolve the zinc sulphate first in most of the water; dissolve the copper sulphate separately in the remainder of the water and filter this before adding it to the rest. Now add the hydrochloric acid and then, while stirring virogously, add the sodium sulphite crystals. The solution may get cloudy at first, but will become clear again if stirred until all the crystals are dissolved. This storage fluid is effective only if kept in a *well-sealed* glass or plastic container and must never come in contact with metal.

To preserve plants or parts of plants without chlorophyl the copper sulphate may be left out.

Toadstools and other fungi may be preserved in the above solution, but can also be stored in 5 per cent formalin.

The traditional way to make dry mounts is by dehydrating the specimen in a glycerine pickle. To make this

pickle take 2 parts glycerine and stir in 1 part acetone and then also 1 part methylated spirits. Plants are soaked in this mixture for a few weeks, then rinsed well in clean water and hung out to dry. Unfortunately this works only with the harder-leaved plants and with twigs of most trees. Herbs, and even trees which lose their leaves easily have to go through one of the following two series:

First, the plants are fixed in the sodium water glass (also called sodium silicate solution) fixative, used above for wet mounting. Then rinse well and leave for one day in the

Bleaching Fluid

Copper sulphate (commercial)	10 grams
Hydrochloric acid (pure, concentrated)	30 mils
Sodium sulphite (crystals)	40 grams
Water	940 mils

The chemicals must be dissolved in the above order. This mixture smells strongly of sulphur dioxide and should therefore be used with adequate ventilation. It cannot be kept, so make it up only when it is needed. Again rinse the plants well and put them for three weeks in

Bath A

Polyethylene glycol 4000	200 grams
Formalin	20 mils
Copper sulphate (commercial)	10 grams
Water	820 mils

After being submerged in this bath for three weeks the plants go, without further rinsing, into

Bath B

Polyethylene glycol 4000	400 grams
Formalin	20 mils
Copper sulphate	5 grams
Water	660 mils

Normally, plants stay in Bath B for three to four weeks but can be left longer without risk.

Polyethylene glycol 4000 (PEG for short) is a water-soluble waxlike substance which can be bought from the Shell Oil Company.

After the plants have been taken out of Bath B they must be rinsed thoroughly in clean water to avoid a surface film of polyethylene glycol. They are then arranged in the right position and left to dry. Especially with very thin or very large leaves this is best done with the entire plant buried in the right shape in clean, dry sand.

It is very difficult to make a dry mount of succulents. The method most likely to give acceptable results is to treat these plants in the normal way with the above fixative, bleaching fluid and Bath A. (The bleaching fluid does not bleach the green colour, but to some extent prevents brown discolouration.) Then after Bath A the succulents are rinsed and freeze-dried as described in Chapter 15.

Many other plants can be freeze-dried without any prior treatment and, in particular, mushrooms and toadstools can give good results.

Bath B is suitable not only for plant preservation but, if the copper sulphate is left out, it also makes an excellent storage fluid for small fishes and other aquatic animals. In that case, to speed up the mixing of the storage fluid PEG 600 may be used instead of PEG 4000. However, PEG 600 is not suitable for plant preservation as it is a hygroscopic, glycerine-like liquid instead of a strong wax.

Some plants show a tendency to shrink in Baths A and B. If that happens, the following series is more advisable:

Fix and bleach again as above, rinse and put the plants *instead of in Bath A*, in

Bath C

Polyethylene glycol	
4000	200 grams
Acetone	50 mils
Copper sulphate	5 grams
Water	780 mils

After three weeks the plants go without rinsing in

Bath D

Polyethylene glycol	
4000	300 grams
Acetone	100 mils
Copper sulphate	2 grams
Water	650 mils

The plants stay in this bath for three weeks and then go in the final

Bath E

Polyethylene glycol	
4000	400 grams
Acetone	150 mils
Water	520 mils

This final bath, which contains no copper sulphate, must act for four weeks. After this bath rinse the plants again, this time in a mixture of 1 part acetone in 6 parts water and dry as above.

The PEG baths of both series can be used over and over again, but must always be kept in closed containers, preferably glass, never metal.

Very interesting and easily-prepared collections can be made of small seaweeds. Blank white index cards are particularly suitable to mount these on. Just float the tiny seaweeds in a plate of water, slip the card underneath and gently lift card and seaweed out of the water together. Any excess water on the card can be blotted away with blotting paper or a piece of blackboard chalk, and the whole left to dry. Normally, the seaweed will stick to the card when dry but a light spray of hair lacquer on the dried seaweed will make it more secure.

To preserve the more fragile seaweeds, float each specimen in a dish of water, slip a piece of stiff paper or thin cardboard underneath and hold the seaweed in place on the paper while lifting it out. Then let it dry on the paper.

Chapter 13

DISPLAY PRESERVATION OF PLANTS

Not always do we need perfectly preserved plants as botanical specimens: we may want small pieces of fern leaves to make a tree fern for a model railway, or a scaled-down pine tree made of pieces of lycopodium; or then again some grasses to go with a mounted bird, or just a twig with leaves for a dried flower arrangement.

In all these cases it will not be necessary to go through the elaborate procedures of Chapter 12. Sometimes, when only a semi-permanent result is needed, it is sufficient to spray a twig of one of the harder-leaved trees with a solution of PVA glue. This glue needs thinning down with just a little water for use with the spray paint outfits which come with most vacuum cleaners. Even an atomiser which can be bought cheaply at any art supply shop will do. Do not worry about the white colour of the PVA; this glue becomes colourless and transparent when it dries.

In autumn twigs of many trees will keep their leaves for up to six months if they are put in a vase with 80 per cent glycerine or a 50 per cent solution of PEG 1500 for several days. When they have absorbed enough of this solution they can be used for normal dried flower pieces or with plumes of grasses or reeds in a container without water. Unfortunately, this method is only suitable in autumn as it rarely works with young leaves or growing branches.

Another method which can be used the whole year round is to bury the plants in borax. Mix equal parts of clean dry sand and borax powder. A layer approximately 1 cm (½ inch) deep is spread out in a light wooden box or even a heavy carton. Arrange the plants in the right position on this layer and gently pour more of the borax-sand mixture between and over the plants until they are just covered.

It is advisable to use a dust mask or at least tie a handkerchief around mouth and nose to prevent breathing in borax dust.

The box with the buried plants is put in a warm, dry place for up to six weeks. The plants will keep most of their colours by this method but the quicker they dry the less they fade. Once the plants are fully dry they can be gently dug up again.

Plants preserved in this manner may be used as they come out of the preservative, but if desired may be touched up with oil paints which have been diluted with a fair quantity of boiled linseed oil and mineral turpentine.

A few of the conifers tend to lose needles. This can easily be prevented by putting the branches in hot water and leaving them to cool down; let them dry again before burying them in the borax-sand mixture, otherwise the borax will form hard lumps which are very difficult to remove.

Many other ideas may be found in books on dried flower arrangements, i.e. killing plants in boiling water prior to drying.

Branches with lichens and many of the harder fungi do not need any preserving at all.

Branches intended for use as taxidermy stands may be left to dry naturally and then treated with a commercial borer killer. One must make sure that a branch is quite dry before mounting a bird on it, or the bird's feet may become mouldy; but if in a hurry dry the selected branch in a fairly hot oven. This will also kill any borer. As an extra precaution the dried branch can be painted with a solution of thymol

If a perspex display jar is made with a curved back, no corners will show inside.

in turpentine and left to dry again. Thymol is an effective poison for moulds and disliked by insects too; it leaves no visible deposit and the unpleasant smell should not be an objection as the mounted bird should be kept behind glass.

If it is desired to make a habitat group for small fish or aquatic insects with water weeds, it is necessary to use the zinc sulphate preservative described in Chapter 12. A very suitable container can be made of perspex; the best shape is a flat box, only a few centimetres deep but high and wide enough to house the selected water weeds comfortably. Cut the panels for this box, including the top, accurately from 4.8 mm (3/16 inch) clear perspex, or alternatively use clear perspex for the front only and take white or opaline perspex for the other sides. The most suitable glue for perspex is Tensol cement, which may be bought from the same shop as the perspex. Instead of Tensol cement we can make a glue ourselves by dissolving a few pieces of clean, clear perspex in chloroform, but this homemade glue is reliable only if we ensure a perfect fit. Whether we use the commercial cement or our own glue it must have a few days to dry completely, and the container must be checked for leaks before use.

The assembly of the habitat group itself is described in Chapter 29. As soon as the display looks satisfactory the top is glued on with the same glue; make sure that no traces of preservative are left on the rim of the container which would interfere with the glueing.

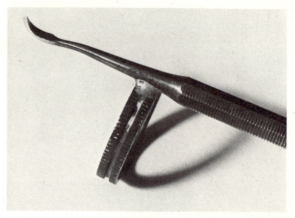

A handy cutting tool for perspex can be made by grinding the point of a dentist probe (scaler) into the right shape. Ask a jeweller to braze on a brass ring to steady the tool.

After cutting along a ruler two or three times, the tool will stay in the groove. Keep cutting until the depth of the groove is between one third and one quarter of the thickness of the perspex, then break off like when cutting glass. Both straight and curved cuts can be made by this method.

Chapter 14

EMBEDDING IN CLEAR PLASTIC

Blocks of crystal-clear plastic embedded with small fishes, flowers or other specimens have become very popular, and rightly so. Material preserved in this manner is easily observed from all sides, and cannot be damaged by insects or by rough handling; it is easy to store and, best of all, the specimens keep their natural colours and lifelike appearance almost indefinitely.

Several plastics are suitable, for example polymethyl methacrylate (of which perspex is made), polyester (used to make fibreglass boats) and also plastics of the ureum family.

All these plastics are bought as clear, syrupy liquids, which solidify after very carefully measured small quantities of two other liquids, the catalyst and the accelerator, have been added. The exact proportions vary with the different brands, and as they are highly critical one must follow the maker's instructions. The catalyst used for polyester fibre-glass work is usually of a very dark colour and would therefore spoil the result. In that case, cyclohexanone peroxide should be used as a catalyst, in the same percentage, usually

in the order of 1 to 2 per cent, as advised for the regular catalyst. Always mix in this catalyst first. The plastic does not set until the accelerator has been added BUT ON NO ACCOUNT SHOULD ACCELERATOR AND CATALYST BE MIXED TOGETHER. These two chemicals are very active and when mixed directly together they may explode spontaneously; yet, by mixing one after the other into the plastic syrup, or monomer as it is called, they are completely safe.

The equipment for measuring and mixing must, of course, be spotless and can be cleaned again with special cleaning fluids.

Although not made specifically for this purpose, resins without fillers or pigments, such as Polymaster (from Consolidated Chemicals), are quite suitable. Even better results can be obtained with special resins such as Celodal (Bayer) and the embedding plastic marketed by Turtox. Turtox has also published a useful service leaflet on the subject.

Almost anything can be embedded, but some species take more preparation than others. Most difficult for a start

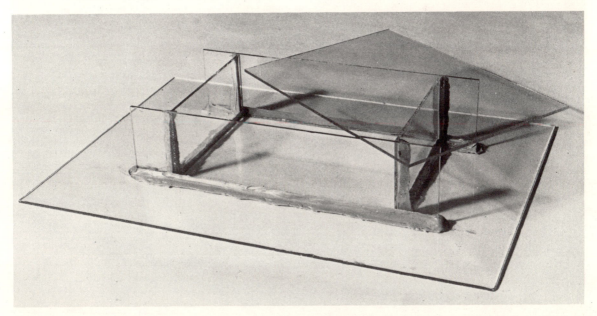

A good mould for embedding is made out of sheets and strips of glass, stuck together and sealed on the outside *with plasticene.*

are butterflies, where without prior treatment the wings may become somewhat transparent; also aquatic animals which are normally transparent but become opaque in the plastic. Beetles also are not easy to do, as without special treatment the wing covers may pull away from the plastic, this giving a silvery-looking result.

The plastic seals in the specimen but does nothing to preserve it, so any animal has to be killed and fixed as in Chapter 10, with flowers dried in sand or in sand and borax.

Many specimens with a dry, fairly rough surface (i.e. a dried starfish, or fossil bones) may be embedded just as they are. Wet specimens such as fish must be left to dry in the air for an hour or so before embedding. When the surface is too smooth, as is the case with the wing covers of beetles, and also with species which tend to become transparent in the plastic, it pays first to soak the specimen for a day or two in glycerine. Wash and dry the surface again before embedding.

A very suitable mould to pour the block of plastic in can be made out of thin glass strips (see photograph). The strips of glass are held in place with sticky tape or plasticine. The mould should be exactly 12 mm (½ inch) deeper than the thickness of the specimen, allowing for sufficient space around it as well. Special release agents are available from the same place as the resin is purchased, and must be painted evenly on the inside of the mould and on a separate piece of glass for the top.

Once the specimen is ready and the mould dry, measure a quantity of resin (enough to fill the mould to a depth of exactly 6 mm (¼ inch), add the right amount of catalyst and stir in gently. Any air bubbles must be avoided, difficult as that may be. Next, the accelerator is added and stirred in evenly. Once the accelerator is stirred in, the plastic will

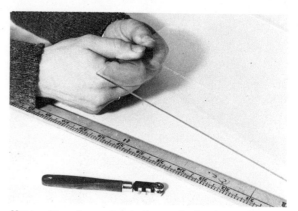

Not too big or heavy glass is then cut by bending one side down at the end of the score mark, as if it were hinged along this mark.

immediately begin to set, so it should be poured into the mould without delay.

The setting time of these plastics depends on the temperature and the quantities of catalyst and accelerator; under 15°C it will not set easily; above 21°C it would set too fast unless we take slightly less catalyst and accelerator.

The plastic will first gel, then get warm and set rock hard.

As soon as the first layer has set, measure a second bath of resin in a clean container, add the catalyst and accelerator and pour another 6 mm (¼ inch) layer: this time arrange the specimen and possibly a label in this layer before the plastic has time to gel. Any air bubbles can be drawn to the surface with a needle or pointed glass rod.

This process is repeated, adding the next layer as soon as the former one has gelled until the mould is just over-full. Then the glass lid is gently floated on top so that the excess plastic runs out along the sides.

After a day in a not-too-cold place the plastic will be sufficiently cured and the mould can be dismantled.

Burrs on the corners, where plastic may have seeped in between the glass strips are removed with a very fine saw and fine sandpaper. Finish off by polishing the whole block with a jeweller's rouge or similar buffing compound or even Brasso on a soft cloth wrapped tightly around a flat wooden block.

The fully cured plastic is, after a few weeks, quite strong, but if it should get scratched badly it can be ground clean again quite easily; use the finest grade carborundum powder mixed into a thin paste with water on a piece of plate glass. The damaged side is rubbed on this paste in a circular motion until it is nicely smooth again. Wash off all paste thoroughly, then repeat on the unused side of the glass with Brasso, or even toothpaste. A final polish with the cloth and the block is as new again.

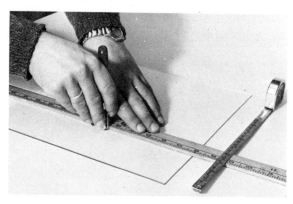

To cut glass score it just once with an uninterrupted steady movement of the glass cutter.

Chapter 15

THE HOME FREEZE-DRIER

Freeze-drying is one of the newest techniques for the preservation of biological material. Big commercial plants are
in use for the freeze-drying of a wide variety of foodstuffs,
ranging from meat and vegetables to coffee and other drinks.
Already in the fifties the Smithsonian Institution in Washing-
ton experimented with the use of this technique in taxidermy,
with very good results.

With the freeze-drying of food shrinkage does not matter,
but our object is to obtain as lifelike a specimen as possible.
The basic principle is simple: the fresh specimen is quickly
deep-frozen in the right position, then placed under vacuum
and kept frozen until it is dehydrated. When the specimen
has just been frozen the ice in the body tissues will keep it
rigid. Under vacuum this ice will slowly evaporate if the
resulting water vapour can be dispersed regularly. With
expensive museum plants this is done by an elaborate
apparatus with a super-cooled condensor and a continuously
working vacuum pump; by the time all the ice in the body
has evaporated, or rather, as it is called in this case, subli-
mated, the dried-out body tissues have become so strong
and rigid that no visible changes in posture or surface texture
have occurred. Although the commercial freeze-driers are
far too expensive for amateur use it is not difficult to make
a cheap but effective home freeze-drier yourself. This gives
perfect results with specimens which cannot very well be
preserved by conventional methods, such as aquatic larvae
of insects, spiders, small fish, many plants and flowers, etc.;
even small birds and mammals mounted by this technique
can be equal to good taxidermy work.

If we have access to an ordinary home freezer we should
have no trouble, but the freezing compartment of the fridge
set at the lowest temperature can give reasonable results. The
equipment is cheap enough, the most expensive item being
the vacuum pump, a water-jet pump which can be bought
for only a few dollars at any scientific supply house. This
type of vacuum pump is a rather amazing gadget; seen from
the outside it is just a T-shaped piece of tube which is
clamped on to the water tap, yet the water jet squirting
through a special nozzle inside sucks the air in through the
piece of pipe protruding from the side with such force that
it creates quite a good vacuum.

We then need some preserving jars of the type with a
metal top, some good quality gas taps and a piece of vacuum
hose. The jars will act as vacuum chambers which, by the
way, we shall use again in Chapter 18. The gas taps are
soldered onto the tops of the jars and the hose connected
to the jars with the pump. Ordinary rubber gas hose is not
strong enough as the vacuum will suck it flat, thus blocking
the air flow.

If you have a little blowtorch you can easily solder a tap
on to a new jar top. Cut off the threaded part of the brass
gas tap and file it quite flat, then drill a hole in the middle
of the top, taking care not to bend it, and scrape the outside
around this hole clean to bare metal; place the tap on the
lid, make the joint well wet with Baker's Fluid or another
good soldering flux and place pieces of tin solder around

Water from mains

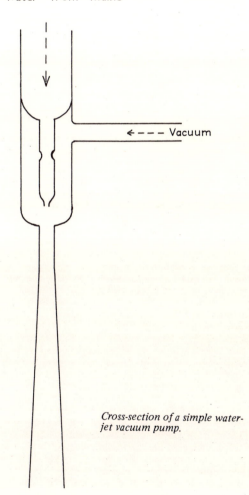

←--- Vacuum

*Cross-section of a simple water-
jet vacuum pump.*

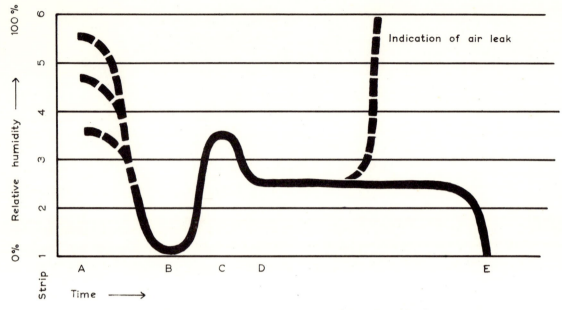

Progress diagram according the colour changes of the cobalt chloride paper strips.

A) Open jar, room temperature: strips 1, 2 and 3 (or more) pink, the other strips blue.
B) Jar filled with layer of calcium chloride, closed and cooled to −15°C: all strips blue, showing that relative humidity has dropped to almost zero.
C) Frozen specimen placed in jar: Strips 1, 2, and 3 pink, strips 4, 5 and 6 blue, humidity of outside air again.
D) Evacuated and frozen properly again: strips 1 and 2 pink, other strips blue. Humidity fairly low, sublimation and absorption of the moisture by the desiccant are in balance and stay like this during the whole process.
E) Specimen dehydrated: all strips turn bright blue.

If during the process all strips turn pink, then this is a clear indication of an airleak, introducing outside air into the jar and thus raising the relative humidity considerably. Evacuate again and reseal the jar.

the joint. When tin solder melts, it always runs to the cleanest spot where there is sufficient flux. Now just play the flame of the torch over the tap, without ever pointing it to the lid underneath, because the tap needs a lot of heat and the top will become hot enough with the tap sitting on it. Also, if you made the top hot, the rubber seal would burn away. Just remember not to touch it while the solder sets again.

If you do not own a blow torch, you will have to ask your local plumber to do this job for you.

When you have a specimen sitting in the jar being preserved, you cannot tell just by looking at it whether the process is finished or not, as it does not change colour or appearance. But I found an easy way out: have you ever seen those picture postcards with a nice blue sky which turns pink when it starts to rain outside? Well, we shall use the same chemical to tell us the condition inside the preserving jar-vacuum-chamber. The chemist can sell us a small quantity, say 15 or 20 grams, of cobalt chloride. Now take six egg cups; the first one is half-filled with water, the other five get one teaspoon of water each. In the half-full one we dissolve as much cobalt chloride as it will take to make a saturated solution. From this saturated solution pour two drops into the first of the other five egg cups, four drops into the second, eight drops into the third, and so on. Thus we get a series of solutions of increasing strength, from very weak to saturated. Six pieces of clean blotting paper, numbered in soft pencil from one to six, are then soaked in

these solutions, number one in the weakest, number six in the saturated one.

These papers now form a very sensitive indicator of the humidity of the air, as they are pink when the humidity is high, but turn bright blue when it gets dry, the weaker ones turning blue much sooner.

Little strips of the paper are glued with just a little dab of plastic glue at the top inside the jar. Space them evenly without touching each other near the top of the jar, so the numbers are visible from outside. Then place a layer of 25 to 50 mm (1 or 2 inches) of fused calcium chloride in the bottom of the jar and close the top straight away. Shut the tap on the top too and our first vacuum chamber is ready for use.

The complete freeze-dry process may sound rather complicated, but in practice you will find it straightforward enough.

First place the well-closed jar in the freezer, so it will be cold by the time we need it; best results are obtained at a temperature of −15°C, or 5°F, which is the same.

Lower life forms, and this includes a number of insects, can sometimes survive complete dehydration, so to avoid embarrassment and an unpleasant experience for the victim, make sure that the specimen has been properly killed. For the best killing methods, see Chapters 10 and 11. Now the specimen has to be mounted in the final position—no special treatment is needed; just arrange it in a lifelike pose on a piece of softboard or cork tile and stick insect pins, and possibly pieces of stiff card on pins around and underneath the specimen wherever necessary to support it or keep it in place. Small birds can have leg wires inserted at this stage.

Put the specimen in the freezer until it is literally frozen stiff. Some insects, in particular many beetles, prove very difficult to freeze; in that case spraying some clean water on them and putting them in the freezer while they are still wet will solve the problem.

Aquatic insects are best placed in a little clean water in a watch glass and frozen in this.

When we first closed the jar, the first strips of paper were probably pink, the others blue, indicating the relative humidity of the outside air. On taking the cooled jar out of the freezer all strips should be bright blue, showing that the moisture in the jar has been almost completely absorbed by the calcium chloride. Open the jar, quickly put some vaseline on the rim, place the *frozen* specimen inside and shut it again tightly.

The vacuum pump, which can have been clamped on to the water tap while the specimen was being frozen (use a good hose clip for this) is now connected with the gas tap on the jar. It is a good idea to place a big preserving jar under the pump as well, so the bottom end of the pump sticks into this jar. This will help us to see when all the air has been pumped out. Open the water tap as wide as it will go and then open the gas tap. Any part of the gas tap, where air might possibly be sucked in, is liberally covered with vaseline to stop any leaks. For a start, lots of air bubbles will appear under the pump, but by the time the jar has been evacuated no more bubbles will come out of the pump. A proper vacuum is essential, so be patient at this stage. If air keeps appearing then there is a leak in the system somewhere; check whether the lid is tight and see if the vacuum hose is properly connected.

When no more air bubbles appear, *close the gas tap*, then, with the water still running, pull the hose off the gas tap and in the same movement plug up the opening of this tap with a fair dollop of vaseline. No gas tap is completely vacuum-proof, but the vaseline will seal it off. ONLY NOW CAN WE SAFELY CLOSE THE WATER TAP.

The actual freeze-drying has begun now, so place the jar in the freezer again and leave it there until the process is finished. If the specimen is allowed to thaw out during dehydration it will collapse beyond repair.

The paper strips will tell what is going on. As soon as the jar is cold enough again the first two strips will be pink, the others various shades of blue. This indicates fairly low relative humidity. The ice in the specimen is slowly "evaporating" and the calcium chloride is absorbing the moisture at the same rate. The process is in balance and should stay so for the time being.

If everything is going according to plan only these two strips remain pink, but it can happen that all strips turn bright pink. This would mean an air leak, introducing outside air in the jar and thus raising the humidity considerably. This will not damage the specimen but it does mean that the jar has to be evacuated once more, and this must be done without the specimen thawing, so put ice blocks around the jar during the "re-evacuation".

Then one day, after a week (or after more than a month, depending on the size of the specimen) we shall see that all the strips have turned bright blue. To play it safe, give one or two more days before bringing the vacuum chamber *back to room temperature* and then open it.

Before the jar is opened the air must be let in, but this

must be done slowly otherwise the specimen would be crushed by the sudden atmospheric pressure.

When the jar is warm and dry again, carefully dig out all the vaseline from inside the gas tap, plug it up again with a piece of foam plastic, tight enough so the air can suck through only slowly and big enough so it will not shoot through the tap into the jar. Now—and only now—can the gas tap be opened.

After all this, which is not really as difficult as it sounds, most specimens come out of the jar fully preserved and completely and permanently lifelike. Only species which depend on a wet skin for their colours, i.e. fish or frogs, will appear a little chalky and pale. However, their colours and general appearance can be brought back quite easily by giving them a few coats of thinned-down clear gloss varnish.

It is advisable to use only fresh specimens for this technique. Alcohol lowers the freezing point of water, as any motorist who uses antifreeze knows, and therefore specimens which have been stored in alcohol cannot be frozen.

The above system is as simple as it can be made and no short cuts can be employed. Water boils at much lower temperatures under lower air pressures (that is why you cannot make a good brew of tea when you climb the Himalayas) and therefore the specimen must be pre-frozen before applying the vacuum.

This also enables you to test your pump and vacuum system; just fill your jar half-full with water at room temperature and evacuate it. If your pump is good enough the water will boil vigorously without having to heat it up in any way whatsoever.

If a specimen which has been freeze-dried is needed for dissecting it can be fully rehydrated by soaking it in a 2 per cent solution of formalin. The formalin bought from a chemist will most likely bear a label stating 40 per cent formaldehyde; in any biological recipe this liquid is to be regarded as 100 per cent formalin, so when it says 2 per cent formalin this means 1 part formaldehyde solution to 49 parts water, preferably distilled or demineralised water.

A freeze-drying jar ready for use.

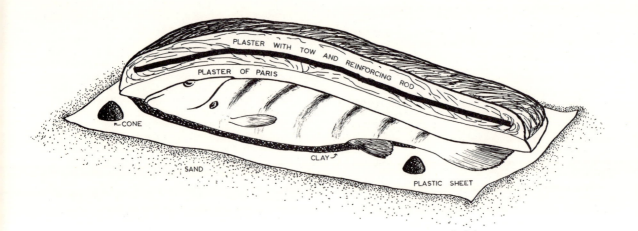

Cross-section through the first half of the mould. A big fish is laid on a sheet of plastic and supported by sand for the first pouring.

A small fish, floating on its side in alginate, ready for the first half of the mould to be poured.

Chapter 16

RUBBER FISH

All the methods we have discussed in the previous chapters have one aspect in common: whether we mounted a bird or dried a plant, whether we freeze-dried a spider or embedded a starfish in a block of plastic, we always used at least an important part of the original specimen, but now we are going to try our hands at something completely different— we are going to make a rubber fish, or in other words, instead of preserving a fish we shall make a cast of one.

Casting may sound very difficult but in actual fact it is a rather straightforward process. First we make a hollow copy of the fish, as a sort of fish-shaped custard form. This is called the mould, but instead of filling the form with custard we use latex and when this has set the result is a rubber fish, or cast.

If it is at all possible, the fish should be kept alive, so we can again make colour notes. Good colour slides are even more useful than they were when we preserved crabs and starfish, and any additional drawings in crayons or paint will come in very handy. I often make these drawings with oil paints, thinned down with some boiled linseed oil; by using these slightly transparent paints on a piece of bright new tin it is easy to get the right silvery appearance.

Don't kill the fish until the colour notes are just right as the colours will fade as soon as the fish dies. Of course, the killing should be done in as humane a way as possible and with no damage to the specimen. Two chemicals are suitable for this purpose. Your chemist will probably not have them in stock but he can order them from the whole-salers. The first one is called tricane methanesulphonate. Dissolve 1 gram in 4.5 litres of water, using seawater for marine fish, and put the live fish in this solution: usually about five minutes is ample. This narcotises the fish but does not kill it. When the fish is properly narcotised it is trans-ferred to a 10 per cent solution of formalin (see Chapter 10). This kills any fish quickly. An alternative chemical which narcotises and kills at the same time is acetonchloroform: a little added to the water in which the fish is swimming is sufficient. After killing, the fish is thoroughly but carefully cleaned of mucus in a lukewarm solution of one teaspoon of alum in a litre (a quart) of water.

When the fish is really clean carefully cut off the pectoral fins (the ones immediately behind the gills) and then we are ready to arrange the fish for the first pouring of the mould. For bigger fish a sheet of thin plastic foil is spread on a layer of sand and pushed down to form a hollow in which our fish fits; place the fish on its side in this hollow, which must be so deep that exactly one half of the body sticks out above the plastic around it; tail and dorsal fins should rest on the

plastic in the right position. Any gaps between the fish and the sheet of plastic must be very carefully filled up with soft potter's clay. It is very important that exactly one-half of the fish is now exposed. As a final step we form half a dozen smooth cones of about 2 cm (¾ inch) out of clay and space these equally around the fish on the plastic. These will later form impressions in one side of the mould and act as keys to fit the two halves of the mould together.

Very small fish cannot be moulded in this way. Here we model a 5-8 cm (2-3 inches) high wall of potter's clay or plasticine onto a sheet of glass to form a sort of dish several centimetres bigger than the fish. From one of the dental and medical supply houses, or if necessary through the chemist, we have procured a tin of dental alginate. This alginate is a material made of seaweed and used to take dental impressions; mix some of this alginate powder with cold water, according to the manufacturer's instructions, but with one-and-a-half times the recommended quantity of water; pour the mixture immediately into the clay-and-glass "dish", making sure that it forms a layer at least half as deep as the thickness of the fish. The alginate mixture will set into a rubbery substance within a few minutes, so at this stage we must work fairly fast. As soon as the alginate begins to thicken, gently float the little fish on its side on the surface and push it exactly half-way down. A number of small clay balls are arranged again around the fish, also half-submerged in the alginate. The cut-off pectoral fins are floated in a little puddle of freshly mixed alginate also and the first stage is finished.

After these few exciting minutes we get a little more time to mix the first batch of plaster of paris. Always use a good quality of moulding plaster. Any body fluids seeping out of the fish would interfere with the setting of the plaster unless we first dissolve a tablespoon of alum per 4.5 litres (gallon) of the water for the plaster; plaster of paris is most easily mixed in a soft plastic bowl or bucket—fill the bucket up to two-thirds at the very most with alum water; now shake up the fresh dry plaster with your hands to loosen the powder and then sprinkle it by the handful into the water—but don't stir. A mound of plaster will build up under the water and eventually break the surface; keep adding more plaster until there is no free water left. I always find it rather difficult not to rush at this stage, but it is best to leave it alone for at least five minutes. After these five long minutes we plunge our hands in the plaster and gently stir and break up any lumps. If you have a sensitive skin it is a good idea to use a barrier cream, as plaster is not very kind to the hands. After stirring, the bucket is gently rocked and tapped to bring all the air bubbles to the surface—skim these off. Then there is another waiting period: for a start the mixture will be fairly liquid, but after a time, depending on the proportions of plaster and water, it will begin to thicken; as soon as it has reached the consistency of whipped cream we must work very quickly again.

During all these preparations the fish should be kept slightly moist with alum water. The great moment to start the first pour has finally arrived. It is best to start pouring on the sheet of plastic or on the alginate, just in front of the head. Pour the plaster out fairly slowly but steadily, in such a way that the edge of the plaster creeps along the surface of the fish just ahead of the place where you are pouring. Try to avoid trapping any air bubbles. The entire fish must be covered, including the cones around it and an area of several centimetres (inches) at all sides around the fish, in one go, with a coat of 2 cm (½ inch) or more. If we are casting a small fish floating in alginate, we simply fill up the clay container to the very top. With bigger fish, however, we have to give it another coat yet. The plaster is mixed in the same way as the first batch, but without alum as it will not touch the fish itself this time. We must, of course, wait until the first coat has set sufficiently before adding the second coat. In the meantime, prepare several loose wads of tow, each about the length of the mould, or less. Tow is flax or hemp fibre, available from any plasterer, and while waiting for the fresh batch of plaster to thicken the entire surface of the first coat has to be scratched to provide a key for the next layer. The wads of tow are then soaked in the thickening plaster, one at a time, and placed on top of the first coat to build up a necessary thickness. With very big moulds, rods of brass or galvanised iron, bent into the right shape, can be incorporated into this layer to give extra reinforcement.

One thing is worth remembering: once plaster has been mixed it sets even under water, so never pour leftovers down the sink—this is guaranteed to block the drains! Just pour it on some old newspapers and let it set where it can do no harm.

During the setting the plaster mould will get rather warm; never handle it until it has cooled down again. Once it is cold again we can safely turn the whole mould over with the fish still inside, to do the other half. All clay and alginate are carefully removed and, if necessary, washed away. Make sure not to lift the fish away from the mould at this stage.

Before we make the second half of the mould a suitable separator must be applied on the plaster surface wherever the two halves will join. The best separator when the mould is to be used for a rubber cast is a slip of potter's clay. Just mix clay with water to a thickish creamy consistency and paint this on the entire plaster surface around the fish. Without this separator it would be quite impossible to get the two halves of the mould apart again without breaking the whole thing.

The second half of the mould is built up in exactly the same way as the first and should therefore give no difficulties. Any plaster that may have run around the first half while we were pouring the second half of the mould may be scraped away as soon as it sets, but apart from that the mould should be left well alone until it has cooled down completely.

The two fins which we cut off at the beginning can be cast in the same way, but will need only one coat of straight plaster without any tow for each half of the mould.

When everything has set completely the joint is scraped clear so the whole joint will be visible as a faint clay line. Sometimes the two halves can now be pulled apart gently, but quite often, especially with bigger moulds, it will be

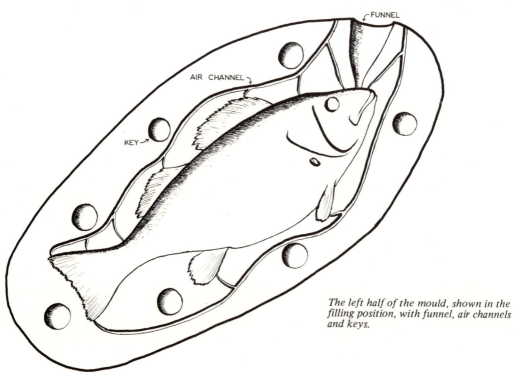

The left half of the mould, shown in the filling position, with funnel, air channels and keys.

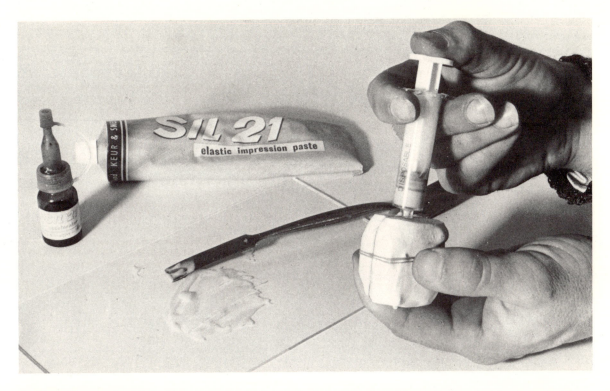

Small moulds are easiest filled with a syringe fitted tightly in the funnel. Continue filling until the material comes out of the air hole at the other end.

necessary to cut fine wooden wedges and lightly drive these into the joint to separate the mould. The fish can then be lifted out, starting at the head.

We now have a hollow fish, but when we examine the mould we notice that there is no way of filling it as it forms a completely closed box, so we cut a half-funnel-shaped channel in one of the halves (see drawing), and also a number of airholes for the air to escape when the mould is filled later. Assemble the mould again and mark the position of the funnel on the inside of the other half. The second half of the funnel is carved out as well, to form an adequate filling hole in the assembled mould.

All plaster scrapings, possible fish scales and leftover clay is now washed out of the mould and the two pieces set aside to dry for a few days, or until just barely damp; however, if the final casting is in rubber the mould should not be too dry. Do the same with the small moulds of the fins.

There are two types of rubber suitable for the final cast. One is a liquid pre-vulcanised casting latex, which any rubber mill can supply, often under the name of glove rubber. The latex types used for gluing are useless for this purpose. The other type is the silicone casting or moulding rubbers. Silicone rubber has the advantage of being more durable, and it does not shrink during the curing. But unfortunately it is far more expensive than natural rubber.

If we decide on silicone rubber we must let the mould dry thoroughly and then paint its entire inside surface with liquid soap or with slightly thinned-down soft green soap. Sometimes two coats may be required to obtain a shiny surface without any visible deposits of soap. The mould is now firmly tied together with string or cellotape and placed

in a cardboard box, or supported in any other way so that the pouring funnel is at the highest point and the cavity inside the mould at a fairly steep angle.

Choose a thin liquid type of silicone rubber and accurately weigh the quantity you expect to need to fill the mould, including the pouring funnel, to the very top. Measure the exact quantity of catalyst according to the manufacturer's instructions and stir thoroughly but gently, so as not to trap any air bubbles. Some air usually does get in, but as most of these silicone rubbers remain pourable for up to half an hour it is possible to let it stand for five minutes to let this air escape. Now pour the mixture into the funnel as quickly as it will run down, keeping the funnel filled to the top all the time; when the whole mould is filled, leave it to set for a day or so.

When a natural moulding latex is used no separators are needed. What is more, any separator on the actual casting surface would cause failures. That is the reason why we used a clay slip as separator between the two halves of the mould itself rather than one of the stronger separators advised in some of the following chapters.

Latex gives the best surface reproduction and the smallest number of air bubbles if the plaster mould is slightly damp. Tie up and fill the mould in the same way as with silicone rubber. Latex does not need any catalysts and can be thinned down with water if it is too thick to pour. The plaster will absorb water out of the latex and leave a deposit of rubber lining the inside of the mould. Just keep the funnel topped up for up to a few hours, when the layer of rubber should be thick enough. The latex, which is then still liquid in the centre, can be poured back and used again. Therefore, when casting in latex, the narrow part of the

47

funnel ought to be wide enough to allow the liquid remainder to be poured off again.

Before the mould can be opened the natural rubber, which is milky white for a start, has to dry to a translucent yellow-brown. With a big mould this may take a few days but can be speeded up by drying in a not-too-hot oven for some hours.

Now the great moment has arrived: the mould may be opened. The two halves of the mould are very slowly prised apart, giving the cast plenty of time to pull free from the plaster. Normally one finds that some rubber has seeped in between the two pieces of the mould and filled up the air channels, so our fish still has an unsightly fringe hanging around it. This can easily be trimmed off with a razorblade.

It will now be obvious why we had to cut off the pectoral fins. If we had not done so they would have been caught inside the plaster and we would not have been able to get them out of the mould. Casting them separately is a simple matter; we do not need any air channels or funnel; just pour some latex or freshly mixed silicone rubber on the deepest half of the mould and slowly lower the other half on top. Excess rubber is then squeezed out and everything left to set.

To glue natural rubber back on to the cast we can use ordinary rubber cement. With silicone rubber, however, we must use a special silicone glue. Silicone rubber is closely related to the material on a non-stick frying pan and therefore normal glues won't stick to silicone rubber.

If we want a really lifelike fish we can make perspex eyes (see Chapter 5) and insert these in carefully-cut holes.

All that is left to do now is the painting: first we give the entire fish a coat of silver paint, or occasionally gold, as the case may be. For the final colouring we use transparent or opaque tube oil colours, diluted with mineral turpentine and a little boiled linseed oil. Never use a too-thick paint, or apply too bright colours, otherwise the result will look very artificial. It is always possible to give another coat if necessary, but washing off is tricky.

Some silicone rubbers do not take paint very easily. In that case make a silver paint yourself by mixing some silver bronze powder with amyl acetate and a little of the silicone glue and use that for the first coat.

After the paintwork has dried completely, give the fish a light coat of artist's oil painting varnish—this will really bring your rubber fish to life.

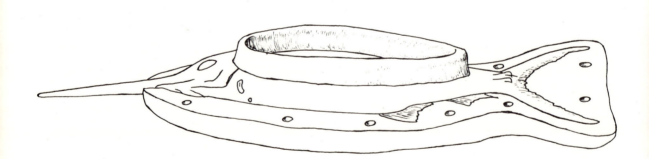

The first half of the mould is finished and turned over. A clay wall built on the now-exposed side of the fish will secure an access hole in the centre of the second half of the mould.

Chapter 17

CASTING A SWORDFISH

Rubber, obviously, is far too floppy to cast anything as big as a swordfish. Plaster of paris can be used—it was used for almost any big fish cast in museums all over the world until fairly recently—but it is both heavy and fragile. So it stands to reason that fibreglass has now become the most popular casting medium.

The first half of the mould is made out of plaster of paris with some alum in the water and reinforced with tow and strong rods, exactly as described for bigger fish in Chapter 16. Many sportsmen prefer to use the original bill in the cast rather than to cast everything, as this makes it more authentic. In that case the mould is made to cover the whole base of the bill, leaving only the slender part sticking out. Of course the bigger the fish, the thicker and stronger the mould must be, with keys in proportion.

Particular care must be taken not to let the fish drop out of the mould when it is turned over to mould the second half. This second half of the mould must cover only as much of the rounding of the fish as will be seen later on from the display side; in other words back and belly will be cast, and the whole area in the middle left open. Build a wall of potter's clay where the plaster should come up to. (See drawing.)

While the mould is drying we cut off the bill just in front of the eyes, at the end of the soft part on top of the skull. The mould must extend far enough beyond this point to enable the bill later to fit firmly with its base in the closed mould. The core of the bill is soft, spongy bone, soaking wet with fishoil. Remove as much as you possibly can of this oily bone with a keyhole saw and wash it out with strong detergent. Proper degreasing is more essential than ever. Use the same mixtures as for tanning, but for longer periods and repeat more often until the bone is completely free of oil.

Most taxidermists use arsenic mixtures for preserving, but as these are rather dangerous to work with I would advise soaking the bill after the degreasing in a fairly strong alum tanning solution (see Chapter 7). Then give it a good rinse and let it dry in fresh air, away from blowflies.

By the time the bill is fully preserved and dry, the mould will be nice and dry too, ready for the separators to be painted on. Fibreglass needs a fairly complex series of separators, the first one being shellac. Fill a jar to the top with ordinary flake shellac, pour in methylated spirits to the same level and leave to dissolve. Apart from being a good separator, this shellac solution also makes a useful varnish and sealer for timber.

Our mould needs two coats of shellac, which can be painted or sprayed on to well beyond the actual casting surface and left to dry.

From a wholesale druggist or a chemist we buy some Carnauba wax, a very hard flaky wax, which we dissolve in enough mineral turpentine to make it into a mixture with the consistency of furniture wax. One thin coat wiped on and brushed out after it has dried is usually sufficient to give a nice shiny finish, but a second coat may improve it yet.

Finally we paint on—spraying is even better—two coats of a special fibreglass separator, available from the same shop as the fibreglass resin. Each of the separators ought to cover not only the actual casting surface, but also the surfaces where the two moulds join, so any spilled resin may be removed before the two halves are joined. Leave everything to dry for twenty-four hours.

Before we start casting we fit the bill for a moment in the *second* half of the mould and mark how far it comes. Use indian ink; ball point or felt pen may stain the fibreglass. Now fit the bill in the first half, place some support under the tip and secure the bill tightly with cellotape.

Two types of resin are suitable, the cheaper one polyester, the other epoxy resin. Polyester is made to set by adding minute but accurately measured quantities of catalyst and accelerator (for details see the maker's instructions and also Chapter 14). Epoxy resin comes in two components, the resin and the hardener. Use either equal parts of each or two parts of resin mixed with one part of hardener, depending on the make. Whichever we choose, it must be a laminating plastic. If one is obtainable, buy a resin without any fillers or pigments and mix in some silver bronze powder *before* adding the hardener, as that will help to get the right colours afterwards.

The first coat, called the gel coat, is brushed on without any fibre reinforcing. Apply an even, fairly heavy coat, but not so thick that it runs down. Most important: make sure you go exactly to the corner of the mould, and never onto the joint.

As soon as the gel coat has set sufficiently the glass fibre mat can be fitted, either a woven fabric or a mat made of chopped strands. Joints are permissible, as long as we let the pieces overlap several centimetres. We can choose a glass fibre mat of medium weight, but although theoretically it depends on the size of the cast the weight is not really critical.

There is no need to mix in any colour for the second coat. Just mix a fresh batch in the normal way and apply heavily over the top of the fitted glass fibre matting. Work it in thoroughly, through the matting and well onto the gel coat. One of those little rollers you buy in the hardware store to cut herbs with will come in very handy to roll in the resin through the glass fibre and to roll out any air bubbles.

If we extend the glass-reinforced coat well into the hollow part of the bill, possibly with two coats to make it even stronger, then the bill will become part of the cast.

The second half of the mould is treated in the same manner, but make sure the plastic does not come any further than the mark for the base of the bill. If you find this too difficult you can always make a little retaining wall of plasticine.

As soon as the plastic has set it should be worked loose from the mould. However, the cast will remain more or less flexible for some time yet, so it must be put back into the mould again after releasing for several more days, to give it a chance to cure fully without sagging. Fibreglass does not reach its full strength until after two or three weeks, but it is quite safe to join the two halves much earlier than that.

The most accurate way to do this is to close the whole mould with the two halves of the cast in position, but alternatively the two sides of the cast only may be cellotaped together for the time being. Now place strips of glass fibre about 10 cm (4 inches) wide along the inside of the joints, with extra care inside the bill. Brush and roll in a heavy coat of resin on these strips and let it set. After a day the cast will be strong enough to handle and to trim off any burrs along the joint.

To fill in any airholes, especially along the joint, we make a puttylike mixture of silverbronze, epoxy glue and possibly some silica flour, or else a ready-made epoxy filler like CIP

emerkit. The same mixture is used to attach the pectoral fins, which have been cast separately (see Chapter 16). The eyes, which for really nice results may be made of perspex instead of being part of the cast, are also put in with this glue.

Once the outside of the cast has been finished and we can tell exactly where the shield on which it is to be mounted should be placed, we cut a piece of 75 x 50 mm (3 x 2 inches) timber, slightly shorter than the hole in the side of the cast and fit this to the curve of the fish. Screw and glue on some shorter pieces to bring it up to the level of the shield. With strips of glass fibre and freshly mixed resin this block is strongly attached inside the cast.

Two more jobs have to be done before we are ready to start painting. First, the eyes have to be masked off carefully with greaseproof paper and cellotape. Secondly, all remains of separator on the fibreglass have to be brushed off with water and the cast dried again; otherwise the separator will separate the paint too.

Pleasant results are obtained if we spray on several light coats of polyurethane varnish with plenty of thinner, only moderately coloured with artist's oil paints. The stripes on the side of a marlin and other colour variations are also put on with the spray gun. The keyword is transparency; at the belly in particular the silvery colour of the cast should not be completely obliterated by the subsequent layers of paint.

Once the paint job looks just right and is hard and dry the cast can be positioned on a varnished shield and screwed on.

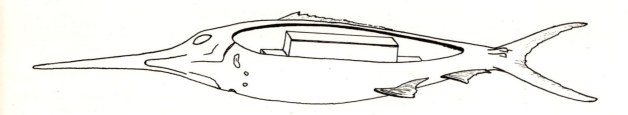

Through the hole in the rear side of the finished cast blocks of timber are fitted inside, the top level with the edge of the hole, to serve as an anchor point when screwing on the shield.

Chapter 18

ENLARGED BIOLOGY MODELS

When natural rubber is soaked in kerosene, it expands to almost twice its size. We can utilise this simple phenomenon to produce greatly enlarged casts of flat objects with an interesting surface structure, i.e. the wing of a dragonfly, or the vein structure of a leaf. Or you can make a 30-cm (1 foot) wide cast in fibreglass of a scale of a fish, accurate in every detail. Casts like these, with an enlargement of twenty-five or more times, are ideal aids when teaching about objects which are normally too finely structured to examine with the naked eye.

What we need is a photographic tray of the size of the desired cast, a supply of prevulcanised rubber without fillers, like glove rubber, some kerosene and plaster of paris, and of course a suitable object, let us say a flat but nicely veined leaf.

Make the leaf wet and lay it, veined side up, on a piece of clean glass. Make a little retaining wall of plasticine around it and slowly pour a layer of about 3 mm (⅛ inch) latex over it, Air bubbles must be avoided at all costs, especially in the early stages, as any defects will be enlarged too and become disturbingly visible. Let it dry in a warm place until the milky white latex has turned into a translucent pale brown rubber. When we remove the original leaf we often find that some latex has seeped underneath. Trim all that away, and also the edges of our rubber disc where the latex may have crept up against the plasticine wall. The top must be flat and the whole rim of even thickness.

Put the disc with the mould-side up on the piece of glass and submerge it in a photographic tray filled with kerosene. Some rubbers expand faster than others and it may be half a day before the mould has grown to almost twice its size. Check occasionally on the size, and when it has not grown any more for an hour or so it is time to take it out again. If we take it out too early the expansion will be uneven. Yet the rubber becomes fairly fragile, and if left too long will be very difficult to handle. Lift it out by the glass and carefully blot the surface dry.

Gently mix a small batch of good quality plaster of paris or even dental plaster. A good way to get rid of air bubbles in the plaster mix is to evacuate it a number of times in the vacuum-chamber-preserving-jar which we used for freeze drying. Air bubbles in the plaster will grow to an enormous size under vacuum and burst when the air is let in again. Pour this de-aired plaster over the expanded rubber mould, starting just alongside and letting the plaster creep along till the whole mould is covered. When the plaster has set and the rubber is removed, we have a sort of plaster dish in the bottom of which is a perfectly enlarged positive copy of the leaf.

This dish is filled with fresh latex again and once more left to dry. From now on the drying of the latex can be speeded up considerably in a fairly warm, but never too-hot oven.

The resulting bigger rubber disc is put back into the kerosene and expanded once more. The system will now be obvious: the rubber negative is expanded, and a plaster positive cast is made of the expanded negative. Of this bigger plaster positive we make a new rubber negative, expand it and cast again in plaster. And every time we repeat this cycle we almost double the size! Thus the fifth stage will give a copy, three-dimensional accurate, in a scale of about 25 to 1, and show details normally completely invisible to the naked eye. We just keep repeating this until we have the enlargement we need or until possible inaccuracies which we may have made in the early stages become too visible as well.

Under no account must we use separators, as these would blur the important minute details which we want in the enlarged copy.

The final cast may be made in plaster of paris, but as the final negative mould was in plaster of paris as well we have to use a separator this time. A mixture of equal parts of liquid soap and raw linseed oil is quite effective, but a coat of shellac in methylated spirits, followed by a thin coat of liquid soap or slightly thinned-down green soft soap will do just as well.

For a transparent object like the wing of a dragon fly a cast in polyester or epoxy resin may be more suitable. The procedure in that case is the same as when we cast a fish in fibreglass, but because of the appearance we cannot use any glass fibre to reinforce the cast. So build up enough layers of pure, uncoloured plastic, without fillers, to get the needed strength.

It pays to keep the whole series of plaster positives until the final cast is ready and satisfactory, so we can go back to a previous stage in case of mishaps. If the plaster at any stage did not run into the deepest parts of the rubber mould, then more than likely some kerosene was left in those corners. If on the other hand the expansion of the rubber mould is uneven or wavy, the disc was either of uneven thickness along the rim or too thick all over. A not-completely-dry rubber may also have behaved in this manner.

The painting of the final cast is straightforward enough: plaster may be shellacked or treated with a commercial sealer first and then painted with any type of paint at all. Fibreglass may be painted as we painted our big fish, or in some cases transparent fibreglass dyes may be added straight to the fresh resin before use.

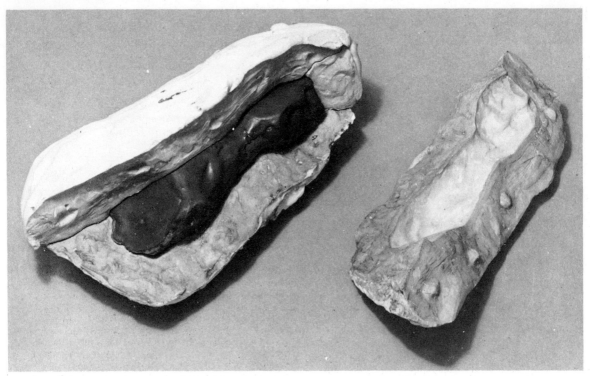

The object is coated heavily with silicone rubber (the mould) and subsequently covered with a supporting shell of plaster of paris (the casing), in this case in four sections. Note the keys where the sections join.

The carved handle of a pre-European Maori bailer. Left the original, right a polyester cast, not yet painted, as it came out of the mould in the previous photograph.

Chapter 19

CASTING ARCHEOLOGICAL ARTIFACTS

So far we have always used a rigid plaster mould to make a more-or-less flexible cast. This was fine as long as we were dealing with objects which were soft enough to take out of the mould without damage. In archaeology this is a different matter, however: if we have to make a mould of a flaked drill point or a rough-hewn adze there would be so many bigger and smaller undercuts where the plaster would get locked in place that it would be impossible to remove the original from the mould without damage.

This time, therefore, we shall make the mould of rubber and the cast in plaster of paris or plastic. We shall make a one-piece mould, covering all sides of the artifact at once, and open at one side only. This opening will of course leave a slight burr on the cast, so we must decide at this stage which position on the cast will make it easiest to remove this burr. Make a note of it, as the mould may afterwards not show the right place as clearly.

We are by now familiar with both silicone rubber and latex; both are equally suitable, unless the artifact is heavily encrusted with clay; some clays affect the setting of some types of silicone rubber.

Paint on as heavy a coat as will stay on, let it cure and turn it over to do the other side. You must work the rubber well into the surface texture without trapping air.

Latex is funny material: if we use a dry brush for it, the latex will coagulate between the bristles and we'll end up with a lump of rubber within minutes. To prevent this, make the brush wettish, rub it on a piece of bland soap and work the soap well in between the bristles before putting it into the latex. This will stop the latex coagulating in the brush and will make cleaning with water and soap later on much easier.

Both latex and silicone rubber stretch too easily on their own and need reinforcing in the *second* coat. Ordinary gauze bandage is wrapped neatly around the artifact with plenty of overlap in one or two layers and fresh latex worked into it. With very big objects a third coat, also reinforced, may be applied in the same way. To get a smooth finish it helps to give it a final coat without any fabric. Let the whole arrangement cure fully before proceeding further.

This type of rubber mould would be far too floppy to use on its own and needs support in the form of a plaster casing. The casing is a shell of plaster of paris in two or more pieces which holds the mould in shape—something like an additional mould, encasing the rubber one.

The plaster is of course completely rigid, so we cannot allow any undercuts which would lock into the casing. The intended joints for the pieces of casing are marked in char-

coal on the rubber, and each piece is checked to ensure that the whole charcoal mark and also the entire surface in between can be seen from *one* viewpoint. If this can be arranged, the piece of casing can be released without trouble. If it is not possible for any one piece, then we have to adjust the markings or even split one of the intended pieces into two sections until every section will be right. Retrace the final markings with a ball point pen.

Stabilise the rubber-covered artifact with props of potter's clay, so the section to be cast first is on top and the marks which indicate the edge of this section are more or less horizontal. Now build a clay retaining wall a few centimetres (inches) wide, well smoothed off and with key holes, with the upper surface exactly along the markings. A clay slip may be applied to the rubber as separator and the whole section filled in with a heavy coat of plaster. When the first section has set, the artifact with the first section still stuck on is turned round to get the second section up. The clay walls are taken away and new ones built along the open sides of this second section. Apply clay slip again on the rubber and—extra thickly—on the plaster where the two pieces join. The last section, of course, does not need any clay walls, as it is cast straight between the other pieces. After all the pieces have been cast, let the whole casing cool down properly before attempting to dismantle it again. So long as we have avoided any undercuts and all the joints have been painted with separator before casting, the casing will now come apart quite readily.

With fine scissors we can now make the incision in the rubber mould and gently, without stretching the rubber, we can peel off the mould in one piece. Cut a round pouring hole of about 12 mm (½ inch) in the mould and if necessary cut some tiny air holes. Put the mould in the corresponding shell of the casing and mark the position of the pouring hole on the inside of the plaster shell. With this marking as a guide, drill and scrape a decent pouring funnel in the casing.

If we close off the base of this funnel temporarily with a plasticine disc we can fill the funnel with rubber, which, when cured, will make a close-fitting plug.

The entire inside of the casing has to be treated now with separator—the normal series of fibreglass separators if we intend to make the final cast in polyester or epoxy resin, or just clay slip for a plaster cast. It is always possible that a little of the casting material will seep between the mould and the casing, and without this separator we would not be able to open the casing.

The long incision in the mould has to be glued shut again very precisely with ordinary rubber cement for the latex, or special silicone rubber glue for silicone rubber. Having the mould sit in one of the shells of the casing during drying helps to keep it in shape.

Assemble the casing with the mould snugly in place and wrap cellotape around it to secure the pieces. Glue the pouring opening of the mould to the inside of the funnel, so no casting material can run in between.

The whole mould arrangement must be propped up with the funnel at the highest point.

If we use polyester or a similar resin for the final cast we must bear in mind the fact that plastics of this type develop considerable heat during setting, which cannot readily escape out of a closed mould. To avoid too-high temperatures we have to reduce the quantity of catalyst and accelerator by at least one half. Better still, we could buy a polyester made especially for casting rather than for laminating.

As soon as the mould has been filled to the top and air bubbles given a chance to escape, the rubber plug is pushed into the funnel to close the mould. Casting material that gets squeezed above the plug won't do any harm and will be easily taken away after it has set.

Give it plenty of time to cure: most casting plastics are very slow-setting. Then dismantle the casing and open the mould again along the glued-shut incision.

Trimming and painting the cast is done in the usual manner. As with the fibreglass fish, dry pigments of the right base colour may be mixed in with the plastic or plaster before casting. This makes the final painting not only easier, but much better.

Silicone rubber moulds have a tendency to absorb small quantities of certain chemicals out of the setting plastic. After five or more casts have been made out of the same mould this may cause loss of surface detail or a slightly wrinkly surface. If this occurs heat the silicone rubber mould for some hours in an oven at about 150°C. This will clear the mould of these chemicals and ready it for another series of casts.

Chapter 20

PULL-OFFS

In the early days of archaeology it was mainly the artifacts which most archaeologists were seeking. By now, however, most amateurs have realised that at an excavation the stratification, the remains of an old fire, a layer of fish scales or a posthole shown by discolouration of the soil may be equally or even more important. Drawings and photographs form an essential record of these, but if the soil were soft enough to excavate with trowel and brushes, the archaeologist could go one step further and take a glued-together slice of the actual face or floor of the pit with him.

When a square has been fully excavated we can apply latex to the most typical face, back this with fabric and pull it free. The whole surface layer of the face, including postholes, artifacts *in situ* and whatever else may be of importance, will come away with it and remain permanently fixed in place.

But you must be careful not to spill any latex on the floor of the pit before the excavation is finished: once when I was making pull-offs during a dig a reporter of a local newspaper found a little dried-up latex in the bottom of a square.

The first layers of latex have been applied to the excavation face above a huge, ancient Maori earth oven.

This completed pull-off, showing alternation of fish-scales and other leftovers from meals; charcoal; bones; tools and many other aspects of occupation layers, covering many centuries of Maori history, has been on display in the Auckland Museum for several years already without showing signs of deterioration.

He interpreted this as dried human flesh and published a report in his newspaper claiming that the people who lived on this site more than a thousand years previously had been cannibals.

By far the best results and the easiest work will be achieved on a warm sunny day. The latex may be applied with a soaped brush, but preferably, if the gear can be brought to the site, with the spray gun of a vacuum cleaner and a petrol-driven compressor or cylinder of compressed air. If there is no alternative latex may be thinned down with water.

For the first coat we cannot use the prevulcanised latex we have been using so far, as that is not sticky enough. Use either *un*vulcanised latex or one of the water-miscible types of latex sold for gluing linoleum. Rubber cement is too difficult to spray or paint on. We can let each coat airdry, but the curing may be speeded up enormously if we spray the still-wet latex thinly with a 9 per cent solution of acetic acid in water. This will make the latex coagulate and the next coat may then be applied straight away.

The next coats have to be strong rather than sticky, so from now on we use only *pre*vulcanised latex. Put on the second coat as heavily as will stay on, and spray again with the acid. This acid is somewhat like artificial vinegar, so quite safe to use.

If there were pebbles in the soil we will find a lot of little but fairly deep depressions in the latexed surface which have to be filled up. Cut small pieces of open-weave hessian, soak these in latex and fill up any holes, curing each piece with acid as we go. For spraying the acid onto these little patches we don't need the big spraygun, as a small atomiser is just as easy. Heavy stones and artifacts *in situ* that are sticking out will need some support in the form of collars of hessian-reinforced latex. This will also help to further level off the surface.

Now cut a sheet of open-weave hessian with an overlap of at least 15 cm (6 inches) at all four sides and drape this over the latexed face. Starting from the bottom, latex is brushed on and worked through the hessian, so that it will stick on to and follow the entire surface without any air gaps. This coat cannot be put on by spraygun.

Make a timber framework with steel brackets in the corners the exact size of the pull-off and place this hard against it. It will probably be necessary to hold it firmly in place with some temporary braces. The hessian overlaps are folded back around the timber and stapled on securely, in particular along the top. Excess hessian may be trimmed away at this stage.

A final coat of latex is applied over the whole pull-off, including the timber frame, and everything is left to cure. This final cure may take several days, even in sunny weather.

Very big and heavy pull-offs, say something in the order of 3 x 1 m (10 x 4 feet) and with big stones incorporated, need the support of a sheet of hardboard as well. This can be clamped against the timber frame just prior to taking it off the face, or better still, fitted inside the frame hard against the rubber surface.

Once we are sure the rubber is fully cured and a translucent pale-brown colour all over we cut through the turf with a sharp knife, 25 mm (1 inch) or less along the top of the pull-off. Now slowly, gently work the pull-off loose from the face, tipping the whole thing back as it comes free. Lift it out of the pit and transport it lying flat on a board, good side up.

Very small pull-offs of fine material only do not need timber frames or boards and may be rolled up after they have been pulled free.

The pull-off can be stored lying on boards in a drawer cabinet or hanging by its frame like paintings or maps in a map cabinet.

By combining pull-offs of the sides and the floor of the same square we can reconstruct an entire excavated pit. Or if we find a posthole bisected by the excavation face the vertical cross section may be combined with the cross section in the floor in one single pull-off. Thus we can make true three-dimensional reproductions of the stratification. In fact they are better than reproductions, for we have taken the originals home.

Chapter 21

RELIEF MAPS

Relief maps may be made for different purposes. We may want a straight-out geographical map, showing the exact elevations in an enlarged scale, painted like a map. Or we may need a more realistic-looking map for use in a classroom, something that looks more like an actual landscape than a map.

The first type is built up out of many layers of thin, easily-cut board, as ivory board or softboard, for example. For strength the base layer can be made of hardboard. We need a map of the right size, showing contour lines. Starting with the lowest elevation each of these lines is traced on a separate piece of board and carefully cut out. At the same time we also trace on every piece the next contour line up. This will enable us to glue all the pieces on top of each other in the exact location.

At this stage we already have a relief map, but terraced rather than with smooth slopes. These steps are now levelled off with sharp knives, rasps and sandpaper, leaving just a little groove to indicate in the finished map the lines of equal elevation. It is a sound idea to make a second relief map, traced off the same map, of the coastal area below sea level. After these two maps have been painted they are glued together with a sheet of thin glass in between to indicate sea level.

For the more realistic-looking map we use a base of expanded polystyrene, also called styrocel. This is the rigid foam plastic used for flowerpots, surf boards etc. It is available in blocks and slabs of almost any size, so it won't be difficult to find a slab of the right size for our map. To cut the outline either a bandsaw or a circular saw are perfect, but an ordinary hand saw or even a sharp knife will do just as well. If used with a sawing motion a sharp knife will give a very smooth finish.

Use a ballpoint pen to draw the whole map on the top of the slab. Several tools suggest themselves for the roughing out—knives or rasps will do. By holding a woodrasp in the gas flame we can bend it with a pair of pliers while it is red hot to make a curved rasp. It will lose some of its temper, however, unless we harden and anneal it again, which is a bit tricky. But the curved rasp will still be hard enough for our job. A wire brush is also very useful for carving plastic. A little disc with steel wire bristles along the rim, it is put in an electric drill. Just touching the plastic with the spinning brush is enough to eat it away at an astonishing rate.

There is yet another, rather surprising tool: a burning match. Hold a burning match just over the surface of the foam plastic wherever we want valleys or lower flats. The heat will melt the plastic, the air inside the plastic foam will

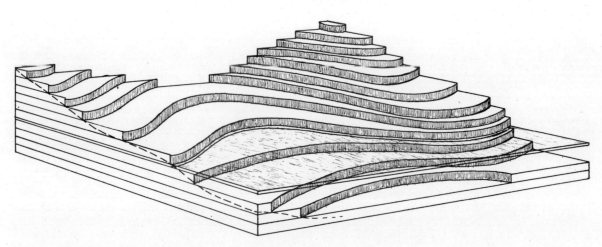

The assembled steps of a layered relief map of a coastal valley with a sheet of glass on top of the fourth layer to represent the sea. The corners of the steps are still to be levelled off to produce a continuous slope as marked on the left side.

escape, and the plastic just shrivels away in the right places!

Each of these "tools" will give a different surface texture, so do some experimenting on off-cuts to get the feel of the material.

Any filling in, smoothing off and further touching up can be done with polyfilla, a white powder which, when mixed with water, sets like plaster. Polyfilla also has a cellulose glue mixed in which makes it stick better, and it is easier to use than ordinary plaster. A final coat of latex will give a nice, smooth finish.

Most plastic fillers and plastic glues as well as non-waterbased paints are incompatible with styrocel. We can easily demonstrate the spectacular results of the solvents of this group if we pour a little paint thinner or acetone on an offcut of the foam plastic. The plastic dissolves, the air escapes and the stuff will eat into the plastic and keep eating! Unfortunately this cannot easily be controlled, so we cannot exploit it.

One of the few suitable glues is a water-miscible PVA glue. This glue is white when still wet, but goes colourless and transparent when it dries and becomes quite waterproof. It can be diluted with water and mixed with dry pigments to colour it if desired.

In a scaled-down landscape the colours have to be "scaled down" too, in other words very subdued colours only are used. Too even colours can be avoided simply by painting several thin coats of slightly different colours and applying the next coat even before the first one has dried. Apart from the brush we can spraypaint with an atomiser—two metal tubes fixed together at a right angle. Just blow through the shorter tube while holding the longer, thinner one in the paint. Again splatter techniques, for instance rubbing a paint-filled

toothbrush on a square of flywire, may be useful.

A seabed or lake is painted green in the shallow and blue in the deeper parts. Some very thin perspex is trimmed to size, painted with clear varnish and a touch of blue oil paint, and then mounted in place as water.

Rockfaces, clay banks etc. are painted in two or three uneven coats straight onto the molten-down plastic; grassland is painted onto a rasped-down surface. A more realistic grass, however, can be made from coloured sawdust. First sift the sawdust to get an even and fine texture. Grass is never plain green, but shows lots of yellows, browns and other colours as well, so we divide the sawdust into four heaps. We then mix three batches of thoroughly thinneddown water-based paints—plastic housepaint is fine—in different shades of green. Pour a heap of sawdust in each bowl of paint and leave the fourth batch of sawdust unpainted. Squeeze out again and let it dry on a sheet of plastic. After drying the four heaps of sawdust are mixed again.

Wherever we need grass the white foam plastic is first painted a dark browny-green. It is then given a heavy coat of PVA glue and sprinkled on a too-heavy layer of the coloured sawdust. Once this glue is completely dry the excess sawdust is brushed away and the grass ready. Possible bare patches won't look unnatural because of the dark undercoat.

Trees and even whole forests can be simulated by gluing on fine lichens, painted in the right colours.

Tiny buildings can be cut with a razorblade out of the same foam plastic, telegraph poles out of the dried stalks of some grasses. Almost any natural material may be used in some way or other, provided all details appear in the right scale.

Chapter 22

MINIATURE LANDSCAPES

Whether the small landscape is to be used at school in a model farm or at home as part of a model railway layout, an important aspect both of the overall design, and the individual details , is the scale. The only way to avoid mistakes, even for the experienced worker, is to make a scale ruler, or buy an architect's one. They are available in almost any scale, from one inch to the foot to one centimetre to the meter.

The base of the miniature landscape can be built out of the same material as the relief maps and in the same manner. Because of the different scale we can show considerably more detail, however, and also make wider use of different surface textures. Very high and pronounced relief, such as a steep mountain with a tunnel, may be built out of glued-together slabs of styrocel and shaped afterwards.

An alternative is to cover a rough framework of light timber and number 8 fencing wire with the finest chicken-wire available. This chickenwire mountain is then finished in plaster of paris or one of the following mâchés. If using plaster of paris, dunk squares of hessian or any other coarse, open-weave fabric in freshly mixed plaster of paris and drape these wet squares with overlaps of not less than 2 cm (½ inch) on the chickenwire mountain.

A good papier mâché is made by unrolling toilet paper into boiling water. Stir and even beat it with an egg beater to make it into an even pulp. Drain, then mix in some dextrine or similar paste. A nice, dense mâché is produced by mixing into the pulp the same weight of rye flour as we had dry paper. Add a little borax to stop it from going off. After drying the rye flour mâché is hard enough to be cut or sawn and sandpapered.

A primitive yet good papier mâché is made by tearing long narrow strips of newspaper, soaking these in any thick paste and gluing them in several layers onto the chicken-wire mountain.

All papier mâchés have to be waterproofed with a good coat of shellac.

One final mâche-like material is a commercial product with the name of Celastic, produced in sheets of different thicknesses. It resembles felt when it is unused. But by wetting it with a special solution, Celastic 1079, it goes very soft, limp and easily shaped before drying strong, hard, and rigid. Use rubber gloves when handling the wetted Celastic. It is sold by the British United Shoe Machinery Coy Ltd.

With the base finished the landscape is built up from the bottom up, first outcrops of rocks and boulders, then bare patches of sand or clay, grass, shrubs and trees. Next come the buildings, fences, powerpoles etc. and finally we populate the scene with people and animals.

Small stones and pebbles are glued on as rocks. Avoid stones with pronounced markings: bright spots or lines may look unimportant in the pebble, but become unnaturally large in the boulder as they won't be to scale.

With the boulders stuck in place the entire scene has to be painted now in subdued dark colours—yellow ochre where sand has to be glued on, raw umber underneath darker soil, and raw umber mixed with chromium green where the grass has to grow. This undercoat should be rather untidily painted. By no means can we use sharply defined, even colours. Spray on the different colours, partly overlapping them so that the brown patches gradually blend into the green or yellowish areas. Work in blurred spots of different shades with a half-dry brush. We need plenty of variation, yet all the colours must be darkish and dull. Bright colours spoil the effect.

Sift the bigger grains out of coarse builder's sand and glue these on for a pebble beach; clay powder will look like sand. For these jobs spray or paint on a coat of PVA glue first, sprinkle on a too-heavy coat of the type of soil we need and brush away the excess after it has dried.

The coloured sawdust of Chapter 21 can be used for a closecropped lawn, but longer grass and tussocks in this scale are better made of borax-preserved, suitable-looking mosses or some of the smallest alpine and other native grasses. Cut these complete with a thin layer of the turf, enough to keep it hanging together. Preserve in the borax-sand mixture in the normal way. After preserving, the roots and left-over soil can be further trimmed away and the little sods glued in place. Extra long blades of grass and seed stalks are cut to length with scissors and some colour added with very diluted paint.

For lakes and rivers we first finish everything under water completely, giving the deeper parts a distinct bluish or greenish colour. Waterweeds made of moss and painted lichens will look very realistic and little fish cut out of aluminium foil are stuck on long pins. Paint the pins a dark, flat colour and they will disappear from view.

The water surface can be made again of thin perspex, varnished with a faint bluish tinge. Duckweed of fine, coloured sawdust can then be glued on the surface. Rapids can be modelled successfully from cellulose acetate. Sheets of this material go soft enough to shape when heated like perspex. Cellulose acetate also becomes pliable for several hours when it is suspended above some methylated spirits or alcohol in a closed jar for one day. It dissolves in acetone, which is useful for gluing.

A thin, old piece of branch, cut lengthwise, will look like an old tree trunk floating in the water when the two halves are glued onto the surface, one piece underneath, the other matching on top.

Many lichens look like scaled-down shrubs and tiny pieces of preserved fern leaves glued together will make convincing ferns. All these things, however, must be checked for size with the scale ruler.

With the whole base finished we may want to add or adjust some colours before buildings and trees are put in. Spraying on a little highly-diluted paint with an atomiser works quite well, especially if combined with very fine brush-work on bare rock faces. And the overall effect can often be improved if the colours of bare sand, grass etc. are touched up by dabbing on some *dry* pigment with a soft brush. The pigment is then fixed in place with a light spray of hair lacquer. (Keep this hair spray off the water, as it dries flat.)

Snow can be made in a variety of ways, ranging from a commercial product that comes in spray bombs, used for window dressing during the Xmas period, to white cotton wool. Cotton wool may be given the slightly translucent look of the refrozen mountain snow by painting some melted white wax over the surface. A hardly visible blue cast in the shadows will give a cold feeling and the whole surface can be made to look more icy with a coat of *clear* shellac. Clear shellac is not as easily prepared as the ordinary flake shellac solution, but may be bought at any artist supply shop.

Just two more points to remember: avoid the use of artificial materials if they can be recognised, for example matchsticks with the head left on for fenceposts. It is wiser to use the finer twigs, with or without bark, of tea-tree or broom. And avoid unnatural tidiness. Put some driftwood on a beach or an old car tyre in someone's backyard.

The bare gumfields north of Auckland form a fine subject for a miniature landscape. To illustrate the scale: the dog was made of the preserved skin of a mouse.

Chapter 23

SCALE MODELS OF TREES

Making scale models of trees is a matter of ingenuity, using the scale ruler, observing the real trees and hunting in bush and garden for materials.

Quite often the seedlings of trees, in particular those of alpine trees, will already look like a scale model of the big tree. A seedling of the New Zealand mountain beech only needs preserving in the borax mixture. If we find the leaves still too big, we can make them look smaller by spraying on diluted PVA glue and sprinkling dark green sawdust on the leaves.

Many of the smaller bonzai trees can be treated in the same manner and make most convincing trees in a miniature landscape.

For the trunks only natural materials can be used, but we have such a wide choice that it won't be too difficult to find the right one. There are twigs, seedlings, tiny shrubs— heaths for instance are very useful—the stems of some ferns and even the woody root systems of many little shrubs may be used.

To make the foliage a wide variety of natural materials may be exploited, for example the husks of grass seeds, lycopodia (club mosses), some lichens, preserved leaves of trees and ferns, and even some manufactured materials as paper or chips of foam plastic may give the right impression.

As the plant materials which can be collected vary enormously with the locality I shall not advise the use of any specific species.

Australian bottle tree
I have never found any shrubs that branched the right way to represent this unusual tree. However, there are a number of shrubs with a root system that looks just right. Any twigs are cut off close to the trunk, which is then mounted upside down. The roots are trimmed to the right length and become the branches of the bottle tree. Soil of course is carefully removed, without damaging the finer roots. PVA glue is sprayed on over the branches and the top of the tree dipped in a bowl of painted and dried grass husks.

New Zealand cabbage tree
The leaves of this tree can be made of preserved blades of grass, but paper is easier and quicker. Cut long, narrow strips, in width the same as the length of the leaves. Paint these on both sides, yellow-brown at one end, green for the rest of the length. Next cut it into the shape of a long comb, the teeth in the form of the leaves. Starting at the green end each strip is rolled up tightly, spiralling down just a little. On the tip of each branch of a suitably-shaped twig we glue

This 50 mm high Queensland bottle tree (Brachychiton rupestre) was made of the roots of some very small sapling. Minute wads of cotton wool, pulled open to become almost invisible, were placed on top, covered very lightly with fine sawdust and secured with hair-lacquer.

one of these little rolls. One by one the leaves are bent down with a needle, the brown ones hanging down along the trunk, the green ones made gradually more vertical, and our cabbage tree is ready to be planted.

Australian grass tree
Again this tree may be made of different materials, small pine needles or tiny tussocks of very small alpine grasses glued together make a good head. But for a very small model of this tree the dried young flowerbud of a thistle stuck on a little twig and sprayed the right colour is all that is needed.

Top: *The baobab* (Adensonia gregorii), *which posed for this 37 mm model, is found in north-eastern Australia.*

Bottom: *The umbrella tree* (Polyscias murrayi), *shown here in a 460 mm model, is a slender palmlike tree growing to about 15 metres. Found on the edges of the rainforests of Queensland and New South Wales.*

Right: *Both the young and the 380 mm mature pine are made of pieces of a lycopodium. The same lycopodium, glued on in a different pattern, can be used to make the New Zealand rimu.*

New Zealand tree-fern

This is one of the easiest trees to make. Some smaller ferns grow a stem that looks almost exactly like the trunk of a tree-fern. And there are quite a number of ferns where the leaves or sections of the leaves are already scale models of the big tree-fern leaves. So all we have to do is collect the material, preserve it, put some colour on and glue the tree together.

Australian umbrella tree

There is a lycopodium that looks like the branches and leaves of the umbrella tree. So once again it is only a matter of collecting and preserving the material and gluing the tree together. The gluing is often made easier by drilling a fine hole down the tip of each branch. It is rather awkward to manipulate a heavy electric drill with a very fine bit. So clamp the drill between two pieces of timber in a vice and manipulate the "tree" instead. Dentist drills are ideal for this purpose. Instead of drilling we can also heat a steel knitting needle in a vice-grip until it is red hot and burn the holes.

New Zealand nikau palm

If we cannot find suitably-shaped and sized leaves, pickle a number of leaves of a broadleaf tree and then cut these to shape with sharp scissors. A good trunk for a palm tree is often difficult to find too. But quite a good result is obtained by wrapping a thread in an open spiral up and down a smooth twig. Cover it all over with PVA glue and paint to achieve the right colour and texture. After the leaves are glued on we model the thick part at the base of the leaves in polyfilla or one of the plastic putties like CIP emerkit.

Pine tree

One of the lycopodia is an exact replica of a pine branch in scale. This lycopodium is very easy to preserve in borax. Stuck on the trunk in horizontal tiers it will produce a Norfolk pine, and with other patterns almost any other pine tree can be made. By hanging tiny pieces from all the tips

of a suitably branched twig the result will look like the New Zealand rimu or red pine.

We may not always need a tree which is recognisable in every detail. If we tear small, rough, umbrella-shaped pieces from a block of styrocel, paint them and glue them on the tips of a smooth but liberally branched twig, we have a stylised gum tree. Twigs of different shapes will in the same way become an oak tree, a cypress or a coolabah, or whatever other tree we like.

Chapter 24

SCALE MODELS OF BUILDINGS

The choice of materials in making houses and other buildings is not really important. What counts is that the final effect is obtained through texture and relief rather than through skilful painting. Not that the paintwork does not matter: it can certainly make or spoil the whole job. But without sufficient relief the painting won't save it.

And, as with any part of a miniature landscape, use the scale ruler to make sure that all details are the right size.

It is easiest to make a house on a strong yet light base: styrocel is again the most suitable. Cut a block in the shape of our house with an electric saw or sharp knife. Don't worry about the eaves, sunporch or other details. The general shape has to be right, but details come later.

The textured surface for the walls and roof is made separately. Weatherboard can be made out of corrugated cardboard. Make it damp with diluted PVA or similar glue and lay it, ribbed side down, on a sheet of plastic or perspex. Press it down with a hot iron so all the ribs are flattened in

the same direction and keep ironing until the cardboard is dry. Cut out pieces to fit all the walls separately, with the "weatherboards" in the right direction. Windows and doors have to be cut out with a sharp razor blade or scalpel. Hold the walls against the styrocel base and mark all the windows.

Before we go any further curtains, blinds, potplants and whatever else may be needed are painted in the window opening on the styrocel against a dark background. Next glue pieces of cellulose acetate the size of the walls on the styrocel base and then stick on the weatherboard walls.

To make an iron roof glue on an oblong of corrugated cardboard with a decent overlap. A house without eaves simply does not look right.

A tile roof can still be made of corrugated cardboard but takes a bit more preparation. First make it damp with very diluted PVA glue. With one of those herb cutters consisting of a number of steel discs on a shaft deeply mark parallel lines across the cardboard, making sure again that the ribs

The framework for a Maori meeting house, or any other building, may be cut from a block of expanded polystyrene.

Work as accurately as you can in the initial stages, but avoid a very tidy and therefore unnatural and sterile-looking finish.

all fold over in the same direction. These marks will be the joints between the roof tiles. The tiles still have the wrong profile, however, so we have to mark them once more, this time with a blunt instrument like a handle of a pair of scissors. Use a ruler to keep this second mark between the first set of lines. Again allow for the eaves when we cut the roof panels to size.

Roughcast walls are made by dabbing a mixture of sand and PVA glue on a piece of smooth cardboard, then assemble as with the weatherboard walls.

A door may consist of a piece of timber, well sanded and with the joints of the planks scratched into the surface, set into the styrocel block. Cut out the appropriate opening in the wall panel so the door will be nicely recessed.

Eaves, window frames, door frames and any other timber parts are cut off icecream sticks with a sharp razor blade and glued in place.

Natural stone may be made straight onto the foam plastic surface. In that case first cut recesses for the windows, paint the window background on squares of cardboard covered with cellulose acetate or directly onto the back of the cellulose acetate film and glue the windows in place. Make a sand-PVA mixture as for a roughcast wall, but slightly smoother. This is painted evenly on the whole wall surface and left to dry. The joints between the stones are marked either by pressure, with a blunt point of a knitting needle, or by heat, with the tip of a light electric soldering iron. This kind of texture has to be painted in at least two colours, the first coat in a cement colour for the joints, but covering the entire surface. The second coat is to be the colour of the stone or a little darker yet. Dab this on with a wad of cotton wool, touching only the high points so no paint runs into the joints. Then, if we want to bring out the relief even better, mix the same stone colour again, but two shades lighter. This last coat is sprayed on very thinly only, from the top of the wall so the jet of paint is just glancing along the surface.

When several houses have to be made it pays to make a mould for the different textures.

Thus a brick wall would be modelled on a slab of plasticine or potter's clay. Make the clay as flat and smooth as possible, then model the pattern of the bricks on the surface in *positive*. This pattern may be impressed with a ruler and a pointed matchstick, but even the milled shaft of a nail punch might give a usable texture by rolling it on the clay.

A thick layer of plaster of paris poured on the positive will make a mould for any number of brick walls. Latex poured on the still-damp plaster mould will set fairly quickly into textured sheets of rubber that can be glued straight onto the styrocel block. Heavy wet paper pressed or rubbed into the mould will retain the impression and may be used in the same manner.

Other materials will find their place in house building too. Some Japanese wallpapers made of natural grasses with a backing of strong paper are just right for the walls of a Maori whare, the roof of which, as for any thatched roof for that matter, is made of tow. A particularly accurate reproduction of the walls of a Maori meeting house can be woven from tow and cotton thread. The primitive little "loom" in the photograph takes almost no time to build and is ideal for this purpose.

No plasticine, oil-putty or other greasy materials should ever be used in a permanent display, as this will invariably result in greasy spots that keep growing.

Painting is essentially the same as with the relief maps: use only subdued colours in flat paints and dry pigments.

Very important also is the joint where the buildings are glued onto the base. Any gap showing there will make it look wrong—it should rather be the other way. Build up the base a little against the walls. Usually the highest plants (and weeds) are growing in these corners.

One final warning: don't include any "smoke" in the scene unless it is absolutely essential to the display story. And if we must make smoke, keep it transparent. Cotton wool is utterly wrong, but two or three partly superimposed plumes of cellulose acetate sheet, made less shiny with hair spray, often do the trick.

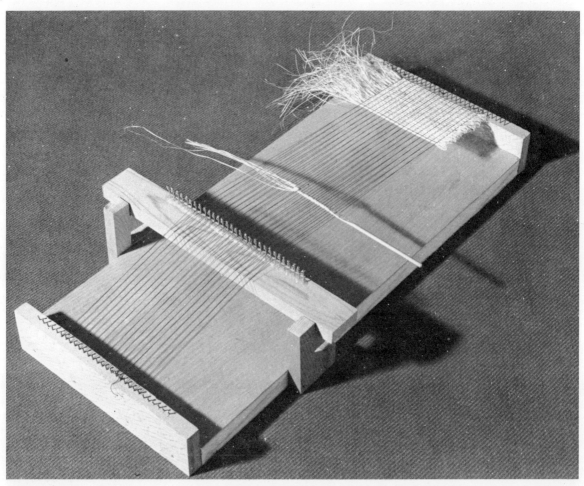

Walls of Maori houses may be covered with material woven on this loom. If the warp gets too tight, owing to the bulk of the hessian or tow woof, use small rubber bands to attach the warp to the little nails at one end of the loom.

A scene at a Maori pa in the days of Captain Cook. The palisades are made of fine, stripped twigs of teatree.

In a scale of 10 mm to 30 cm we can already show considerable detail, as demonstrated in this gumdigger scene.

Chapter 25

SCALE FIGURINES

No scene is complete without people or animals. How to make these depends on the scale and on the number required. If we need only a few not too small-sized, modelling the figures on a wire frame is the most logical way. Bend a figure like the famous drawing of "The Saint" in thin iron wire. Leave the legs about 12 mm (½ inch) too long. This extra length can later be pushed into the base to anchor our men in place.

Whether we make a detailed iron wire frame for a bigger figurine or a simple frame of fuse wire for a very tiny one, the leg wires must always be left long enough to be pushed into the base of the display.

The actual modelling can be done in a whole range of materials. The rye flour papier mache works well for bigger figures, of say 4 mm to every 10 cm (½ inch to the foot). A man in this scale would be between 70 and 75 mm (2¾ and 3 inches). For figures of that size we can sew clothes from very fine linen. Use plain linen only and paint in the right colours

after the clothes have been put on. Of course the mâché figure has to be shellacked and painted first before being dressed.

Instead of the rye flour papier mâché an asbestos mâché is very pleasant to work with too. Make a very strong solution of animal wood glue and mix in enough plaster of paris and ground asbestos, in equal quantities, to make a stiff putty.

For smaller figures a finer-textured material is easier to use, i.e. polyfilla mixed with paint, or one of the plastic putties. For a temporary display a modelling wax is just as successful.

Modelling waxes can be mixed to show different properties. A wax that is hard when cold but becomes malleable after being slightly warmed and kneaded is made by melting together eight parts of beeswax, one part of rosin and one part Venetian turpentine. This Venetian turpentine is a syrupy rosin, available through most wholesale chemists. Nothing else can be substituted: if we were to use mineral or vegetable turpentine, we would end up with a type of furniture polish instead of a modelling wax.

Another type of wax which should be brought up with a brush while melted consists of four parts beeswax, five

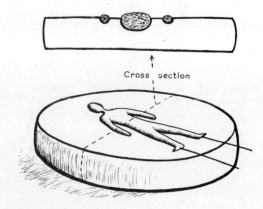

A cross-section shows how far a one-piece mould ought to be overfilled to obtain a nicely rounded small figurine.

parts rosin and one part Carnauba wax. Keep the wax just melted in a waterbath so that each brush stroke of wax goes hard as soon as it is brought up.

Figurines in each of the above materials have to be shellacked before painting.

It pays to make a mould where a bigger number of figures is required. The simplest mould is the one-piece mould in plaster of paris. Model the full, three-dimensional figure on its back on a sheet of plastic in plasticine, clay or modelling wax. Pour the mould in plaster of paris or, for very deep profiles, in dental plaster.

Moulds for very tiny figures, say in the order of 12 mm (½ inch), may be carved straight into a slab of plaster. Take an impression in plasticine occasionally to check progress.

15 and 25-amp fusewire are ideal to make the wire skeletons for smaller figurines. The pieces of wire are twisted together for a few turns in the middle as body, then bent apart and down again through the arms. The leg wires must be longer than the legs in order to pin the men down.

By using a flexible material for the cast the wire skeleton will make it possible to give the figures any pose we may need.

No separators are needed if we choose a prevulcanised latex, preferably with a high content of filler. First put the skeleton in the mould, then the latex. Overfill the mould somewhat to avoid flat back sides. Silicone rubbers do not shrink and therefore give better results, but they require a light soap separator. Papier mâché may also be used. All mâches need a heavy oil or wax separator, but may be taken out of the mould long before they are dry.

Bigger figures look better if made in a two-piece mould. The technique ought to be clear by now. The initial figure is modelled in an easy straightforward pose in wax or plasticine. A wide pouring funnel or a cylindrical rod the thickness of the nozzle of a syringe is modelled underneath the feet. Making the mould and the actual casting involves the same process as for very small fish in Chapter 16. A wire skeleton is placed again in the mould before casting. A dental silicone rubber may be used too. These dental impression materials are made to set in an extremely short time—too short for

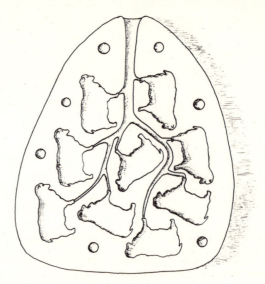

One half of the mould for a Christmas tree of sheep. The air vents have not been drawn in to avoid confusion.

our work. But if we take only half the prescribed quantity of catalyst then we shall have just long enough to put the mixed silicone rubber in the syringe (without needle) and inject it into the mould until it begins to squirt out again through the airhole at the other side.

If we have a really big number to do then we make several casts from the initial mould, arrange these casts all joined to a common pouring hole and make a new mould of the whole set-up. Each cast from this new mould will now produce a kind of Christmas tree of men or cattle.

Captain Cook and his men, visiting a Maori settlement. By casting the 25 mm-high figures in a flexible silicone rubber they can be given any pose. Only five different moulds were used for the entire group.

Chapter 26

SCALE MODEL OF A HORSE

The ultimate in scale models is reached when it becomes impossible to tell from a good photograph whether we are looking at the original or the model. We shall now try to reach this peak by building a horse with a real hide. A good scale is 4 mm to every 10 cm (½ inch to the foot), which makes it one-twentyfifth of the real size. The manikin is made as a scale model, and the finishing off is plain taxidermy.

The wire frame will be fairly complex this time and will have to be soldered together. First cut two pieces of light galvanised iron wire, preferably new, about four times as long as the horse model. Twist these together for a few turns as spine, and bend the free ends down as legs. The legwires ought to be long enough to stick in a temporary styrocel base to make work easier. A third piece is looped double as head and twisted onto the spine with the free ends. There will be no tail wire, but the finest galvanised wire available has to be wound around the whole frame, fairly tight around the legs, with big, tight loops alternating along the spine and a little tighter again along neck and head. This will provide an anchor later on for the modelling wax.

Before we attempt the final adjustments to the frame the wires have to be soldered together everywhere. A good wash with warm water and soap will get rid of the remainders of flux that otherwise would cause rust-stains.

Good photographs are essential and if we are lucky enough to find some the same size as our model it will be a great help.

The frame must be bent to fit exactly inside the future horse. It can't be adjusted afterwards, so make sure that the wires will remain below the projected skin surface by at least 3 mm (⅛ inch). Pay extra attention to the proportion of length and height and details like the direction in which the head is held. Note also how close to a square the overall proportions of a horse are.

Once the frame is perfect from every angle the manikin can be built up and finished in one of the modelling waxes of Chapter 25. Every blemish will show through the skin, so keep modelling and smoothing off until pose and finish are faultless. Put in taxidermy eyes or small beads and give the whole manikin two or three heavy coats of shellac.

The skin will have to come from two or three white rats, cleaned according to normal taxidermy techniques and preserved for about ten minutes in saturated borax-water. Put some dextrine on the manikin as body paste and put the first skin on the back immediately after preserving. Don't give the skins time even to begin to get hard, as that would make the work much harder. A rat does not have enough of a horse-shape to do the whole mount in one skin. There-

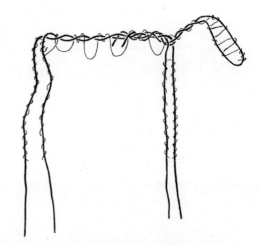

The wire frame of a horse.

fore keep the joints as well trimmed and well hidden as possible. Use insect pins to keep the skin in place where necessary.

With a little trimming the rat's ears can be used for horse ears, the aluminium foil of a milkbottle top is thick enough to use as stiffening.

First with a wet paintbrush of hog-hair, then with a wet sable brush the hair is combed and brushed into the right pattern. The hair pattern of a horse is completely different from that of a rat, so refer to the photographs all the time. While skin and fur are still wet it is easy to adjust the hair, keep brushing till all the hair lies smoothly in the right pattern.

Let the horse dry now for several days. Then spray and if necessary brush on enough alcohol to make the skin soaking wet. This will harden the skin and set the hair. Let it dry again.

The insect pins which were used to keep the skin in place may now be removed.

If you still dare to face your chemist you have to go and buy some good, strong hair dye in horse colour or a shade darker. Quite possibly it will take two washes of dye before the colour is dark enough, unless you prefer a white horse. And again, make sure the hair pattern is still right while it dries for the last time.

The mane is made by gluing on a narrow strip of fox skin or similar fur and the tail can even be a bundle of human hair.

Paint hooves and lips, and a horse has been created.

In any kind of scene it is of the utmost importance to make the transition from the three-dimensional display (here the section with the mounted birds) to the painted background as invisible as possible.

Chapter 27

BACKGROUND PAINTING

In order to get a completely realistic-looking background to our model landscape the painting must be a continuation of the three dimensional part in colour scheme, scale and general atmosphere. Sharp corners must be avoided, as these break up the smooth flow of the painting and utterly destroy the illusion.

The most successful shape for a backdrop is a full dome, gradually curving into the three-dimensional foreground to make the transition less noticeable. However, a full dome is hard to construct and even harder to paint. We shall restrict ourselves therefore to a straight up-and-down background, curved horizontally only.

First make a light timber frame, with studs of 90 x 30 or 60 x 30 mm (3 x 1 or 2 x 1 inches), depending on the size and no more than 30 cm (12 inches) apart. The noggins ought to be cut to the right curve before nailing them in. Clamp and then nail a sheet of *thin* hardboard to the frame. Ivory board (a type of thick cardboard) may be used instead but, although it is easier to handle, it is far less strong. Ivory board needs a coat of shellac to seal it. Punch in the nails, putty up with plastic wood and sand smooth so no marks will show in the finished painting.

At this stage there is still a sharp corner at the joint between foreground and backdrop that has to be made far less visible. Fill in this corner with damp sawdust, tow or even crumpled-up newspapers, covered with a layer of papier mâché. A thin sheet of Celastic is ideal for this purpose too. This curve must be so gradual and smooth, without any marks, that it becomes impossible to tell where the foreground ends and the background begins. Plaster of paris is not suitable here as it is certain to crack away from the board behind. Touch up and fill in with plastic wood where necessary and sand it all down nicely.

The board is fairly absorbent and needs a coat of sealer, followed by a full coat of a good primer-undercoat, right down to the foreground.

The background painting, both in colour and in design, is controlled to a great extent by the final lighting conditions. So before doing any more to it we have to go through the next chapter and install the lights.

We are used to seeing the horizon at very near eye level, but we cannot make this a definite rule in display work. Often a compromise gives a better impression. If we get a disproportionately high section of painted landscape by taking the painted horizon up to eye level then we distort the continuation of the three-dimensional part into the painted part of the display. And this continuation is certainly the deciding factor. Put the horizon therefore where it looks best and sketch in the rest of the landscape.

If at all possible some three-dimensional parts should be included in the painting. A mountain in the same scale as those in the foreground, modelled in strong relief directly onto the background in papier mâché or similar modelling material, or alternatively a silhouette building put just in front of the backdrop, can do amazing things.

Watch one point though: a straight or vertical line drawn on the curved part of the backdrop does not necessarily look straight and may have to be drawn curved to appear straight.

Shadows in the sky look very odd, so wherever a tree throws a shadow onto the backdrop, sketch in another tree exactly coinciding with this shadow to make it disappear.

When the sketch cannot be improved any more it is time to put in the so-called underpainting. Fill in the approximate colours of the landscape fairly thinly, in oil paints, diluted with mineral turpentine only.

Next paint in the sky, whitish near the horizon and becoming a deeper blue when we get higher up. Finish the sky completely, with one or more thick coats. We don't want a shiny surface that would cause reflecting highlights in the sky, so no linseed oil should ever be used in this type of painting. Dilute the paint instead with a little turpentine and perhaps some flat oil varnish.

With the sky finished and dry, the landscape itself can be painted. Start in the far distance, gradually painting away from the horizon and finishing the objects in the foreground last.

We don't need a wide range of oil paints to make the colours needed, with the following list virtually any colour can be mixed—flake white, ivory black, cadmium yellow, cadmium red, mars orange, yellow ochre, raw umber, burnt umber, cerulean blue (for the sky), cobalt blue, viridian green, and oxide of chromium green.

Everybody knows that blue and yellow give green. With the two greens of the list and the yellow we already have two ranges of green. But black mixes in a similar way to blue, so black and yellow give a range of olive-greens. And black or blue with yellow ochre produce many bronze-greens. Paler greens can be obtained by adding some white. We already had two greens straight from the tube that can be mixed in as well. And seeing that any number of colours may be mixed together at the same time one will be hard put indeed to think of a green that cannot be mixed from the above list.

The mixing of browns may seem somewhat confusing for a start, but once we know that yellow and red give orange, and orange and black make brown, then it makes sense that if we add some red to olive-green (black and yellow) we also get a brown. There is a distinct difference between the orange made from cadmium yellow and cadmium red and the bought mars orange. The latter is already browner and gives therefore a second range of browns. Yellow ochre and cadmium yellow may both be mixed either with raw or burnt umber or both. Then of course we can mix red (or orange) with, for instance, burnt umber to produce different reddish browns. There is literally no limit to the number of browns that can be mixed from just these few tube colours.

Greys are made from black and white and can be used to tone down the intensity of any of the other colours.

The enormous freedom and variety in mixing oil paints may be somewhat overpowering at first, but after some experimenting one soon gets the feel of it.

In a painting of this type one must never use pure colours straight from the tube as they would be much too bright. All colours must be mixed to the right shade under the final lighting conditions. Don't worry if a colour looks wrong in the painting. We can easily mix in more colours straight into the wet paint on our "canvas" to adjust the overall colour scheme. Any details that won't come right can be repainted straight over the top or wiped away with a rag moistened with turpentine.

The general colour scheme must match the scene in front as well as possible, gradually getting dimmer and more subdued as one gets more into the distance. Far mountain scenes show a distinct cobalt blue haze. Keep the shadows in the painting in the same direction as in the foreground and also extend the painting down the curve into the three-dimensional section.

Sandy patches, some vegetation etc. may be extended a little into the painting in turn, to make the transition less abrupt. Mountains and whatever else may have been modelled in relief onto the background are painted in the same colour as those in the three-dimensional part, to make them come forward from the flat part of the painting and thus add still more depth.

After the painting has dried we will most likely still find some shiny patches that reflect light and to some extent disturb the illusion. Just spray or brush a coat of flat varnish over the whole scene and all will be well.

And finally, if the transition of three to two dimensions is still not perfect, we can do some careful blending with dry pigments.

The overall lighting comes from a suspended fluorescent tube, held in place by 40 mm terry clips. The sunlight is produced by one or more floodlights, with metal baffles around them to mask off stray light and restrict the yellow light to carefully selected areas without overlapping. The whole arrangement is concealed from view with a removable panel.

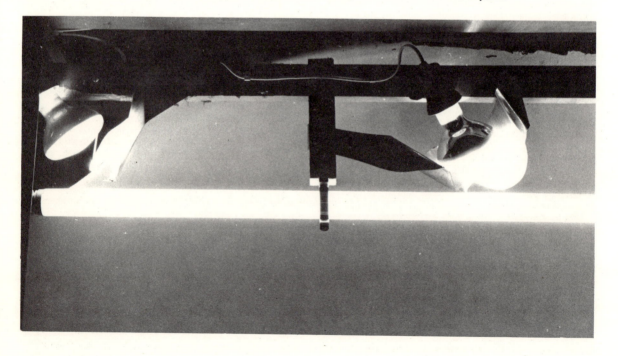

Chapter 28

LIGHTING THE LANDSCAPE

We have gone to great pains to make our landscape as natural-looking as possible. Yet there is one aspect we have not touched upon so far: light. Artificial light, if it is arranged properly, can really make the whole scene come to life, but done incorrectly, it can in a subtle way make it appear like an unsuccessful imitation.

On a sunny day (a sunny landscape always gives the most effective impression in miniature work) we can see two distincly different colours of light. I am not talking of the colours of the spectrum into which the light can be separated with special instruments, but what can be seen with the naked eye. We have the highly directional and clearly yellow light of the sun, but in contrast to this the bluish and completely diffused light thrown down in every direction from the blue sky. Diffused means from every direction, therefore having no recognisable direction at all.

On the sunlit side of any object the yellow light dominates, making the colours yellower and brighter; in the highlights on shiny surfaces the yellow may even drown out other colours. In the shadows, of course, we have no yellow sunlight at all, only plenty of diffused blue light, giving a noticeably different colour pattern. Shadows therefore show a distinctly blue cast. Follow this colour pattern also in the background painting, with the painted sunlight coming from the same direction as in the three-dimensional foreground. And if our landscape represents a well-known existing scene, take care to put the sun in the right place in the sky.

In lighting technique and photography the colour of the light is called the colour temperature and is given in degrees Kelvin. The Kelvin scale works with the same degrees as Celsius, but starting at absolute zero, the lowest temperature possible. If a theoretical "black body" is heated, then it will first get red hot and emit red light. Next it will become yellow, white and finally blue-white. To give the overall colour temperature of any light we give the temperature to which this black body must be heated to emit the same colour light.

The light from the blue sky varies quite a lot with the time of the day, but for display purposes we may safely take it between 4500° and 6000° K. Some fluorescent tubes give light of this colour. Tubes made in New Zealand go by code number, suitable ones for sky light being code 55, with a rating of 6500° K. and 33, with a colour temperature of 4200°K. The choice between these two is a matter of taste; .an in-between colour, for instance, may be obtained by placing a 33 tube underneath a blue reflection screen. Other tubes give wrong colours, the 27 for instance is yellowish, the 35 too pink. This is easily demonstrated if we paint a nice, subtly blue sky under the proper light and then replace a tube with a 35 tube.

A few tubes, spaced widely apart, give a well-balanced diffused light.

Incandescent lights may be used instead of tubes, provided they are bulbs of the floodlight type and placed behind a filter of blue cellulose acetate. Shops for stage materials supply special filter material. A big reflection screen must be mounted horizontally above the display, the floodlights placed low and with the beams shining on the screen only. They must of course be hidden from view and no *direct* blue light is allowed to fall onto the landscape. Incandescent lights produce more heat than fluorescent tubes, so allow enough space for ventilation.

Sunlight cannot be simulated with tubes as the light would not be directional enough. For a smallish display one floodlight placed beside the end of the backdrop will be fine. Any sunlight falling on the painted sky or the reflection screen above must be screened off with a baffle near the light bulb.

The intensity of the light falls off with the distance: an object shifted to twice its distance from the light source will then get light with only one quarter of the intensity. A very wide landscape may therefore not receive enough sunlight at the far end. In that case we have to install two suns, one alongside and a second further towards the middle, both beaming down at the same angle, but baffled off so the sunlight of the two sources does not overlap. These baffles must be placed very accurately: double shadows look rather alien.

The standard fluorescent tubes are made to be run off the mains only, but regarding the incandescent light bulbs we may well prefer low voltage types, say 12-volt.

To understand the advantages of a low-voltage system we have to have another small dose of theory.

The three main units to measure electricity are the volt, the pressure behind the electrical current; the ampere, which, to keep it simple, we can say measures the quantity of electricity; and lastly the watt, the product of volts and amps, or the energy produced by pressure and quantity combined. Volts x amps = watts.

A floodlight bulb is more or less mushroom-shaped. The flattish front is slightly diffusing to avoid harsh circles of light, the back of the bulb is internally silvered to focus the light into a fairly wide, soft-edged beam. Spotlights look the same, but give a much narrower beam of higher intensity.

The smallest 240-volt floodlight is 60-watt, which makes it 0.25-amp. and the biggest 12-volt flood is 50-watt, or more than 4-amp. This means that the "quantity" of electricity going through the filament of the smaller 12-volt bulb is more than sixteen times greater, resulting in a whiter, more intense light from the 12-volt bulb. Yet, because the 240-volt lamp has to handle a much higher, more potent and dangerous "pressure", its physical size is much bigger. What this means in simple words is that for a big display, where we need a lot of light and we have enough space to install the bigger and hotter 240-volt lamps, with something like 150-watt bulbs, 240 volts are fine. But for a smaller landscape, when we get into the lower wattage range, or if it is difficult to conceal the lights and yet keep adequate ventilation, then the 12-volt system is much better. Low voltage is also far safer to handle and the lamps are much cheaper. The only drawback is that we need a transformer or car battery for the power supply. Choose a transformer big enough to supply all the power we need with some to spare so it won't get overloaded. It is not safe to run three 50-watt lamps off a 100-watt transformer.

Normal fluorescent tubes cannot be hooked into the 12-volt system. They come in a variety of sizes and in some lengths are available in two different wattages. But, as with incandescent lamps, the smaller sizes become progressively less efficient and give less light per watt. When we get into the really small sizes then the nice, slender *miniature* fluorescent tubes are ideal. They usually come in four sizes, ranging from 15 cm (6 inches) - 4-watt - to 53 cm (21 inches) - 13-watt. The quality of the light is good and they are far more efficient than low wattage filament lamps: a normal 240-volt/ *40-watt* lightbulb gives less light than the 30-cm (12-inch) *8-watt* miniature tube!

Always make sure your installation complies with the regulations of the local electricity board. Use sufficiently heavy cables of the right type: even with low voltage a too-light cable will overheat and cause fires. Don't build any dangerous makeshift arrangements, but hook up your wires with special connecting boxes and attach all cables with the proper aluminium strips. The right kind of cable has three wires, each with a different colour insulation. In New Zealand these colours are red (danger!) for the phase or live wire, black for the neutral "return" wire and green (safe) for the earth wire, which is connected to the metal parts of any appliance as a kind of safety valve.

Chapter 29

LIFE-SIZE HABITAT GROUPS

Even the best-mounted piece of taxidermy work still looks unnatural unless it is in its natural surroundings. If the purpose of the mount is no more than identification, then a completely neutral background won't interfere. And if the only reason is to show the size, then the trophy mounted on a shield has already become so much a tradition that most people can accept it without further thought.

However, if we want a specimen to be more than just another trophy, or if we want to use it for teaching, we can improve it no end by placing it in its natural surroundings or habitat.

We usually know where and how our specimen used to live in its wild state, so it is just a matter of picking the most characteristic part of its habitat and reconstructing it.

A starling likes living in a built-up area, so if we mount him on a piece of lawn in front of a brick wall it won't look out of place. Preserving a reasonably big sod of grass, cut with a thin layer of the turf, is something we know now how to do, and the brick wall background is made of styrocel. Take a big slab with a rough-cut surface, mark the bricks with ballpoint pen and melt in the joints with the tip of a heavy electric soldering iron, trailed along a metal ruler. Paint the whole slab with a heavy coat of dark brick-coloured water-based paint, followed by two thinner coats, neither quite touching the entire surface, in two lighter, slightly different colours. The mortar to be placed (not too tidily) into the joints is a mixture of sand, grey paint or pigment and somewhat thinned-down PVA glue.

A freeze-dried gecko may be put half-hidden between preserved vegetation appropriate to the place where it was caught, but to make it more visible in the classroom it may be put on some boulders to sun itself. These boulders can again be made of styrocel; a coat of latex put on prior to painting will get the best texture. Also several layers of soft-board, glued together, cut and sanded to shape and finished in the same manner will make fine stones. The boulders should be left flat on the underside to glue them onto the base. Glue on soil between the stones, as in the miniature land-scape, so the stones will look half-embedded and let some grass and other plants "grow" between them as well. Make lichens on the boulders from only partly-mixed very thick paint, dabbed on with an overfull brush.

A kingfisher may be mounted on top of a post or at the entrance of its nest in a hole, dug in a bare, long-dead tree trunk. Or we can reconstruct its nest as it is sometimes found as a tunnel in a riverbank near the sea. Any of the techniques used to make miniature landscapes may be employed, the only difference being that this time every detail must be life-size.

Underwater scenes can be made in two different ways. Bigger scenes are best kept as a dry reconstruction. Fishes are then cast, starfishes dried, sea centipedes freeze-dried and so on (see Chapter 10). Seaweeds are exceedingly difficult to preserve well and are better cast in fibreglass. Boulders may be made in the now familiar way, but if we want barnacles and similar growths, then either use the real thing or make a cast in fibreglass of the originals. A rubber mould of a bigger rock-face with barnacles, tubeworms, limpets and whatever else you may find growing on it can be made during low tide and cast afterwards in fibreglass at home. Only animals with too high water content, like sea anemones and jellyfish are better reconstructed entirely. Use cellulose acetate film (as for the rapids in a miniature land-scape) or perspex (see Chapter 5) to mould the body and paint only very lightly with transparent paints on the inside.

The three main characteristics of any underwater scene are that nothing looks wet, that the light is utterly diffused without sharp shadows, and that the background gradually disappears into a blue haze. This haze is reconstructed success-fully by inserting one or two sheets of perspex, painted evenly on both sides with thin blue-tinted semigloss varnish, into the scene, one in the middle, the second about three-quarters of the distance from the front. Conceal the edges between boulders, seaweed etc, so the sheets cannot be recognised as such, leaving only the hazy effect.

When dealing with very small material, from a little pond for instance, then a wet-mount display is quicker to make. Waterweeds, very small fishes, insects, etc. can all be pre-served in one and the same preservative, as described in Chapter 13. The only thing to watch for is that the pre-servative in question contains some hydrochloric acid which would dissolve calcium. Therefore shellfish cannot be incorporated in the display. And what is more, if there are any pieces of shells in the sand we intend to use on the bottom, then they have to be removed first. So sift out big pieces of shell first, then wash the sand thoroughly. Next pour some hydrochloric acid over the sand in a deep glass or plastic container and repeat it until fresh acid stirred through the sand does not cause it to foam up any longer. Then wash the acid out and put the still-wet sand in the bottom of the display container.

Next fill the container almost up to the top with freshly-made-up preserving liquid and arrange waterweeds, fish and other specimens nicely. Fish may be tied onto a thin sheet of perspex or suspended from very thin nylon threads. Suitable threads may be pulled out of fine, light-coloured nylon stockings or sometimes from very lightweight nylon fabric. Even human hair may be used.

Don't wait too long before sealing the container, but leave an airspace under the lid to allow for expansion of the liquid with changing temperatures.

If a flat, hazy-blue background does not give the right effect an underwater background may be painted separately and glued onto the outside behind the container.

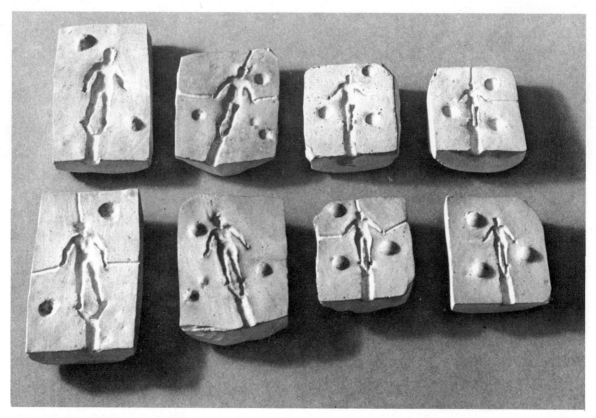

The original mould of a very small figure (left) and three subsequent stages of mould-shrinking, to produce even tinier casts. Note the filling funnel, air holes and keys.

Chapter 30

TABLETOP PHOTOGRAPHY

All the displays we have made in this book are eminently suitable for tabletop photography. No fish will pose as patiently as a mounted fish, and in no landscape can we let our imagination roam as widely as in our own self-made miniature landscape.

The subject material is unlimited and the requirements but few: apart from a camera all that is essential is a stable tripod and a double-range exposure meter.

Any camera with which we can take time exposures will do, but most suitable are single lens reflex or plate cameras. With double lens reflex cameras and with cameras with a separate viewer we get "parallax", which in particular on a short distance can be quite noticeable. Parallax means that the view of the main lens and that of the viewer lens don't quite coincide. Still, by measuring the distance between the main lens and the viewer it becomes simple to allow for this while positioning the camera. What the camera "sees" and will take, will be the above distance lower, or lower and to the right, from what the viewer shows.

The main problem is usually the limited depth of field. The closer we bring the camera to the subject, the narrower the strip that is in focus becomes. Therefore if we have the choice between different lenses, select the one with the narrowest angle, or in other words, with the longest focal distance, even a telelens, and take the shot from a fairly long distance. If the lens cannot be changed, it may be necessary to get sufficient depth of field by taking the photo from a longer distance. In that way some of the room around the subject scene, and also part of the table underneath will probably appear in the shot too, but it is simple to enlarge only that part of the negative that shows the scene we want and thus get perfect results.

The depth of field can also be increased by selecting a smaller diaphragm (with a higher number) and a correspondingly longer exposure time. Don't overdo this though: going to really small disphragm openings, 16 or 22, sometimes impairs the overall sharpness of the photo.

If the scene is built specially to be photographed rather than as a nature study table or a model railway layout, it is an excellent idea to measure the depth of field first and construct the scene within these limits. The illusion of such a shallow scene is made much stronger by applying the laws of perspective in the modelled part also; by using, as it were, painting techniques in a three-dimensional way. Instead of making the buildings rectangular, build them on a shallow diamond-shaped plan. In addition have everything, buildings, trees, people etc. bigger in the immediate foreground, gradually scaling them down until they are very tiny near the painted backdrop.

I developed a simple way to cast different-sized figures from the same mould. We have already used the expanding rubber system to enlarge figures, but in this case it would be rather tricky to model the very small figures in the far distance sufficiently accurately to allow for expansion. It is much easier to model the biggest ones first, where we can still see what we are doing. Model the men the normal way in wax or plasticine and make a two-piece mould in plaster of paris. Before using this master mould to cast any rubber figures, and while the plaster is still damp, make one cast in dental alginate. An alginate like the dental impression compound CA 37, made by Keur and Sneltjes, is perfect for the purpose if it is mixed with one-and-a-half times the normal quantity of water. Alginates like these will shrink if they are left to dry after setting.

If we have difficulty casting the alginate figure a little soft soap may be used as separator, but don't mask out any detail. The alginate figure is now left to dry somewhat, though never completely, until it has shrunk to the desired size. Let it shrink to, say, about 85 per cent of the original size. If extremities such as arms tend to dry too quickly, keep them damp with little wads of wet cotton wool. As soon as it has shrunk to the right size, make another plaster mould of it. From this second mould we make another alginate cast and keep repeating the process. In this way we end up with a whole range of moulds in diminishing sizes which can be used to make silicone rubber men in the normal way.

The normal camera is not quite as adjustable as the human eye, so allow for just a little more contrast in the painting of both fore- and background.

The general lighting can be the same as described in Chapter 28, with one exception. Colour films are balanced for either daylight, or artificial light, i.e. incandescent light, and cannot cope with a combination of the two. So if we intend to use our scene for colour photography and we are not very experienced in the use of colour-correcting filters, it is far wiser not to use tubes but only incandescent light bulbs, and to select a good artificial light film.

Wet-mounted underwater scenes present another problem—reflection in the front panel of the container. However, this is not impossible to overcome. First of all, keep the room as dark as possible, except around the display container itself. Avoid any light that may reflect from the front of the container into the direction of the camera. Diffused light on the container, masked off with baffles to keep the rest of the room in the dark is best, but if that is not practicable two slide projectors placed at some distance, one at either side of the container so the shadows cancel each other out, will often give just the right quality of light. Next drape a big black curtain in front of the camera, with a small hole cut in the middle through which to take the photo. Angle the display container just enough to stop the reflection of the camera lens poking through the hole in the curtain from showing in the front panel, and we are ready to shoot.

Reflection screens to adjust the lighting further in a tabletop scene can be made of any kind of board, painted white or covered with crumpled-up and then slightly straightened-out aluminium foil.

If there is a visible light source in the photo, a lamppost or a miniaturised 12-volt "table lamp" in an indoor scene, a campfire or the headlights of a car, then we have to make sure that the light in the photo seems to come indeed from this light source. Normally the light source will be too bright in comparison to its surroundings, causing a bright white point in the photo, surrounded by a faint halo and then black. So we bring in a supplementary light source outside the scene, with a screen with a hole cut in it directly in front of the light, so that it seems to radiate from the light in the scene itself.

Even with the additional lighting the light source in the scene may still be too sharp. If the camera allows it we can overcome this by taking a double exposure. First take a shot, with all the lights on, of half the required exposure time. Now switch off the visible light source in the scene and, without moving the camera or transporting the film, we take the shot once more, this time with half the exposure time which would be required under the new conditions.

Focussing on a dimly-lit scene is often rather difficult, so put an extra bright light above the scene that is temporarily switched on during the focussing only.

Sometimes a birds-eye view looks fine, but the great majority of tabletop photographs are far better when taken at eye-level.

We have gone to a lot of trouble and spent many hours, admittedly enjoyable, on preparing the scene, yet taking the photo may require less than a second. Why not play it safe at this final stage and take three shots, one of the presumably correct exposure time, one of half, and one of double this time? Then at least we are sure that we have one shot that has been worth all our effort.

Good luck.

Appendix

NOTES ON PROTECTED ANIMALS

Australia

Australia

Almost all native birds and mammals are protected throughout most of Australia. However, widely varying wildlife laws exist in the different States and careful enquiry concerning these laws should be made to the relevant authorities. Addresses for enquiry are as follows:

Australian Capital Territory
The Director, Agriculture and Stock Section, Department of the Interior, CANBERRA, A.C.T. 2601

Northern Territory
The Director of Animal Industry, Northern Territory Administration, DARWIN, N.T. 5790

Territory of Papua - New Guinea
The Director, Department of Agriculture, Stock & Fisheries, KONEDOBU, T.P.N.G.

Queensland
The Director-General, Department of Primary Industries, William Street, BRISBANE, Queensland, 4000.

New South Wales (including Lord Howe Island)
The Director, National Parks & Wildlife Service, 2nd Floor, ADC Building, 189-193 Kent Street, SYDNEY, N.S.W. 2000.

Victoria
The Director, Fisheries & Wildlife Department, 605 Flinders Street Extension, MELBOURNE, Victoria 3000.

Tasmania (including Bass Strait Islands)
The Secretary, Animals & Birds Protection Board, G.P.O. Box 422E, HOBART, Tasmania 7001.

South Australia
The Director, Department of Fisheries & Fauna Conservation, G.P.O. Box 901E, ADELAIDE, S.A. 5001.

Western Australia
The Director of Fisheries & Fauna, Department of Fisheries & Fauna, 108 Adelaide Terrace, PERTH, W.A. 6000.

New Zealand
Under the Wildlife Act 1953 (and supplementary legislation) practically all native birds are absolutely protected, including migrants, such as cuckoos and godwits and species which arrive here by accident, whether they become established or not. Apart from native birds, animals absolutely protected are the rare native frogs, tuatara, and the long-tailed and short-tailed bats. On the other hand the only bird *introduced by man* which is given absolute protection is the white swan. Provision is also made under the Act for the partial protection of some birds, while others are declared to be game (i.e. may be taken under licence in certain seasons).

Glossary

alginate A powder that sets quickly when mixed with water to make very accurate rubbery moulds. Not suitable for moulds that are to be kept for more than a few days.

aspirator A vacuum cleaner-like gadget for collecting insects.

atomiser Extremely simple and cheap spray paint gadget, consisting of two metal tubes joined at right angles.

balsa An extremely light, soft kind of wood.

body paste A thick, gluey mixture which helps to slide the preserved skin around the manikin and afterwards hold it in position.

brain spoon Long, slender spoon-shaped scraper.

carnauba wax A hard wax with high melting point, extracted from the leaves of a South American palm.

clay slip Potter's clay, diluted with water to a creamy consistency.

diaphragm In photography: the mechanism to alter the lens opening of a camera.

diorama A completely realistic looking scenic display, either lifesize or in scale, with a three-dimensional foreground merging into a two-dimensional background.

dowel A round wooden rod, available in a range of diameters, commonly used for jointing timber in cabinet making.

dry pigment The finely powdered colouring agent used in paints. Most pigments mix readily with water (not so some blacks, in particular black oxide) but are not water-soluble. They must never be confused with powder paints, as dry pigments contain no binding agents whatsoever. A mixture of pigment and water cannot be used as paint unless we add some PVA as well.

epsom salts Common name for magnesium sulphate.

ferrule The metal tube holding the bristles or hair of a paintbrush.

fibreglass Synthetic resins, usually polyester or epoxy resin, reinforced with fine glass fibres.

fillers Inert powders as silica flour, Omnia G, cork powder, or even soot, mixed in with plastics and rubbers to improve certain properties, alter consistency or generally increase quantity.

fluorescent lamp A tubular lamp without filament, filled with a gas that under the influence of an electrical discharge emits U.V.-rich light, that in turn makes the fluorescent powder at the inside of the tube radiate bright light in the visible part of the spectrum.

forceps Straight or curved tweezer-like instruments, with tips in a wide range of shapes and sizes.

glue size A fairly weak solution of organic glue in water.

incandescent lamp An electric lamp where the light is produced by a brightly glowing filament.

keys Small knobs and corresponding depressions along the joints of a more-piece mould to facilitate locating the sections when assembling the mould.

latex The raw material of which natural rubber is made: the sap of certain trees, treated chemically to stabilise it.

maceration Softening and near-liquefying of organic material by steeping in a suitable fluid.

manikin Artificial body for specimens mounted by taxidermy methods.

narcotising Rendering an animal unconscious in a gentle, gradual manner.

perspex Trade name for an extremely clear plastic (polymethylmethacrylate), sold mainly in sheetform, also coloured, called plexiglass in Europe.

sable Hair of a small carnivorous mammal, the marten, used for high-grade artist's brushes.

scalpel Small surgical knife.

silicone rubber A synthetic rubber-like material.

tow Flax or hemp fibre.

turf A dense, fairly hard peat, cut in blocks, dried and sold as fuel.

undercuts Depressions in the original in such positions that they would lock a mould onto the cast if both mould and cast were made of rigid materials.

whiting A pure, finely powdered chalk.

Index

Acknowledgments

I am most grateful to Mr E.G. Turbott, Director of the Auckland Institute and Museum, for his encouragement and generous advice during the writing of this book, and for permission to use museum materials and displays for the following photographs: 1, 14, 15, 24, 25, 26, 27, 28, 35, 36, 37, 38, 39 and the cover photograph.

I am also indebted to Mrs R. Shannon, who helped by typing the manuscript, and to the New South Wales National Parks and Wildlife Service and the Division of Wildlife Research C.S.I.R.O. for information on the legislation relating to wildlife protection in Australia.

Bibliography

Leon Pray, *Taxidermy.* Macmillan Co., New York, 1967. This book is suitable for beginners, the techniques are based on the use of borax as preservative.

John W. Moyer, *Practical Taxidermy.* Thames & Hudson, London, 1953. Suitable only for the more experienced workers.

The Australian Museum, *Hints to Collectors: Birds* (Leaflet No. 57, June, 1961). The Australian Museum, Sydney.

Other Reed Craftbooks

Spin Your Own Wool
Molly Duncan

An introduction to spinning and weaving, giving concise instructions for home spinners and beginners, followed by a section of home dyeing with direction for use of onion skins, lichens etc. for bases, as well as chemical agents.
48 pages, many diagrams and photographs, cased.

Creative Crafts With Wool and Flax
Molly Duncan

Following on from the author's spinning text, this book gives detailed hints for planning threads, knitting with homespun wool, weaving with wool yarns, flax and its threads, colour, and embroidery in flax and wool. Of interest to art and craft teachers, this is the first book to give instructions on flaxwork—especially useful for rural schools.
64 pages, profusely illustrated, cased.

Dollmaking for Pleasure and Profit
Gwynne Nicol

The whole process of designing, making and dressing dolls is detailed in this illustrated craftbook. With the addition of a chapter on doll-marketing which will encourage professional dollmakers, this book has wide appeal to students, teachers and hobbyists.
64 pages, many diagrams and illustrations, cased.

A Guide to Flower Arrangement
Margaret Watling

A practical step-by-step guide to many forms of flower arrangement, with special reference to the seasons and flowers of Australia and New Zealand will be useful to flower arrangers at home and in the office. The many photographs and drawings of flower arrangements will help both professionals and amateurs to create fascinating and original arrangements.
64 pages, line and photograph illustrations, cased.

Dyes from Plants
Joyce Lloyd

A detailed description of equipment, supplies, methods, dyestuffs and tie-dye will give the newcomer to this field an ideal starting-point. Information about dyes from native plants of Australia and New Zealand as well as from common vegetables and weeds used in dye processes will be valuable to anyone interested in dyes.
48 pages, many diagrams and pictures, cased.

Pottery for Pleasure
Elizabeth Lissaman

The author gives guidance on New Zealand and Australian clays and raw materials, along with information about and descriptions of clay preparation, pottery with and without a wheel, decoration, colouring, glazing and firing.
56 pages, profusely illustrated, cased.